# THE POPULAR JEWISH BIBLE ATLAS

# Reuben Turner

# THE POPULAR JEWISH BIBLE ATLAS

## From Abraham to Bar-Kochba

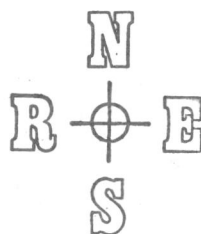

JCP **Jewish Chronicle Publications**
25 FURNIVAL STREET, LONDON EC4A 1JT. Telephone: 01-405 9252

Design and Art Work: Rivka Aderet-Myers
Cartography: Lorraine Kessel

Copyright © 1986, Reuben Turner and Carta, Jerusalem

ISBN 0 900498 90 0 ✓

Printed in Israel.

# TABLE OF CONTENTS

## MAPS

PAGE NUMBER

1    IN THE BEGINNING

Introduction ................................................. 7
The Nations of the Biblical World ................... 10
City Building After the Flood ........................... 11

2    THE PATRIARCHS AND
     THEIR WANDERINGS
     2000-1500 BCE (Before Common Era)

Abraham's Journey to Canaan ......................... 12
Haran at the Centre of Trade Routes .............. 13
Abraham, Isaac and Jacob ............................. 14
Joseph and His Family Go Down to Egypt .... 15

3    MOSES AND THE EXODUS
     FROM EGYPT
     1300-1200 BCE

The Struggle Between Egypt
and the Hittites ......................................... 16
The Exodus from Egypt ................................. 17
The Conquest of Transjordan ......................... 18
What Moses Saw from Mount Nebo ............... 19

4    JOSHUA AND THE CONQUEST
     OF CANAAN
     c. 1200 BCE

The Battle of Jericho ................................... 20
Joshua's Conquests of Canaan ........................ 21
The Land of Canaan ..................................... 22
The Twelve Tribes ....................................... 22
The Sea Peoples .......................................... 23

5    THE DAYS OF THE JUDGES
     1200-1025 BCE

The Judges ................................................. 24
Deborah's Victory Over Jabin ......................... 25
Incursions from the Desert ............................ 26
Samson and the Philistines ............................ 27
The Philistines Capture the Ark
of the Covenant .......................................... 28
Samuel's Judgeship ..................................... 29

6    THE KINGDOM OF SAUL
     1025-1010 BCE

Saul's Exploits Against Israel's Enemies ...... 30
The Battle of Michmash ................................ 30
Saul's Kingdom c. 1025-1006 BCE    ............... 31
David and Goliath ....................................... 31
David's Flight from Saul ................................ 32
Saul's Battle Against the Philistines ............. 33

7    THE KINGDOM OF DAVID
     1010-970 BCE

The Kingdoms of David and Eshbaal ............. 34
David Conquers the Philistines ...................... 34
David's Conquest of Jerusalem
c. 1000 BCE    ........................................... 35
David Expands His Kingdom ......................... 36
The Kingdom of David .................................. 37
Absalom's Rebellion Against David ............... 38
The Battle Between David and Absalom ........ 38
Sheba's Rebellion Against David ................... 39

8    THE REIGN OF SOLOMON
     970-930 BCE

Solomon's Kingdom ..................................... 40
Solomon's Foreign Trade .............................. 41
The Districts of Israel Under Solomon .......... 42
Solomon's Jerusalem ................................... 43

9    THE DIVISION OF THE
     KINGDOM
     930-880 BCE

The Division of the Kingdom ......................... 44
Rehoboam's Fortification of Judah ............... 44
Shishak's Campaigns Against Judah
and Israel ................................................. 45
The Conflict Between Asa and Baasha .......... 45

| 10 | THE RISE OF ASSYRIA AND THE FALL OF ISRAEL 880-721 BCE | Battles Between Aram and Israel | 46 |
| | | The Defeat of Assyria at Qarqar | 47 |
| | | The Campaign of Shalmaneser III 841 BCE | 48 |
| | | Damascus Conquers Transjordan | 49 |
| | | The Kingdoms of Jeroboam II and Uzziah | 49 |
| | | Attacks on Judah | 50 |
| | | The Fall of Israel | 51 |
| | | Population Exchanges under Tiglath-pileser III | 51 |
| 11 | THE FALL OF JUDAH 721-587 BCE | Judah at the Time of Hezekiah | 52 |
| | | The Assyrian Empire | 53 |
| | | The Babylonian Empire | 54 |
| | | The Captivity in Babylon | 55 |
| | | Nebuchadnezzar's Campaigns in Judah | 55 |
| | | Judah After the Exile | 55 |
| 12 | EXILE AND RETURN 587-332 BCE | The Fall of Babylon and the Return to Zion | 56 |
| | | The Persian Empire | 57 |
| | | Jerusalem at the Time of Nehemiah | 57 |
| 13 | THE RULE OF GREECE 332-167 BCE | The Empire of Alexander the Great | 58 |
| | | Alexander's Successors: The Ptolemies and Seleucids | 58 |
| | | Greek Cities of Antiochus' Realm | 61 |
| 14 | THE MACCABEES AND THE HASMONEAN DYNASTY 167-63 BCE | Judas' Campaigns Outside Judea | 62 |
| | | Judas Maccabeus Revolts Against Antiochus | 62 |
| | | Essene Settlement at Qumran | 63 |
| | | The Hasmonean Family Tree | 64 |
| | | The Expansion of Judea Under the Maccabees | 65 |
| | | The Empire of Alexander Janneus | 65 |
| | | The End of Jewish Independence | 65 |
| 15 | THE RULE OF ROME 63 BCE-CE 6 (Common Era) | Pompey's Conquest of Jerusalem | 66 |
| | | Pompey's Division of Judea | 67 |
| | | The Parthian Invasion | 67 |
| | | Herod's Kingdom | 68 |
| | | Herod's Jerusalem | 68 |
| | | The Dead Sea Sect (The Essenes) | 69 |
| | | Herod's Kingdom Divided | 69 |
| 16 | THE REVOLTS OF THE JEWS AGAINST ROME CE 66-74; 132-135 | The Kingdom of Agrippa I CE 44 | 70 |
| | | The Jewish Revolt Against Rome CE 66 | 71 |
| | | Jewish Military Regions After CE 66 | 71 |
| | | The Roman Attack on Jerusalem CE 70 | 72 |
| | | Vespasian Conquers the Galilee and Judea | 72 |
| | | The Conquest of the Last Rebel Strongholds | 72 |
| | | Judea Between the Revolts CE 73-131 | 73 |
| | | The Outbreak of the Bar-Kochba Revolt | 74 |
| | | Suppression of the Revolt | 74 |
| | | Ancient Sites in the Holy Land | 75 |
| | | Index | 76 |

# INTRODUCTION

Through the attractive coloured maps and concise text, THE POPULAR JEWISH BIBLE ATLAS provides an informative and interesting introduction to the study of the Bible and the early period of the Jewish people.

No other book is so widely read as the Bible, and no other volume has made a greater impact and contribution to humanity and civilisation.

The Bible's teachings proclaim the eternal truths that human society must be based on goodness, kindness, justice and righteousness. At no time more than the present is there a need for these lessons to be understood.

REUBEN TURNER

# "IN THE BEGINNING"
### *(Genesis 1-11)*

The story of mankind begins with God the Creator creating a perfect world filled with plants, trees and shrubs, animals, birds and planets, light and water. Man and Woman, the only ones who were created in the "image of God", were placed at the apex and centre of creation with the capacity and capability of understanding and gaining knowledge. It is in the area of Mesopotamia, between the rivers Tigris and Euphrates, that the narration about the beginning of the Universe unfolds. Genesis describes how God dealt with men and women and the world in which they lived. It speaks about the origin and meaning of Man and Life. The Bible was never intended to be a book of science or a text book on history. It shows the relationship between God and mankind and how through God's commandments a person can best conduct and live the God-given life.

So the Bible commences by relating how the first pair of the human race, Adam and Eve, were placed in the magnificent Garden of Eden where every living thing lived in harmonious serenity. Adam was to live and work in the

JAPHETH

SHEM

*R. Tigris*
*R. Euphrates*

*Mediterranean Sea*

NOAH

*Arabian Desert*

HAM

*R. Nile*

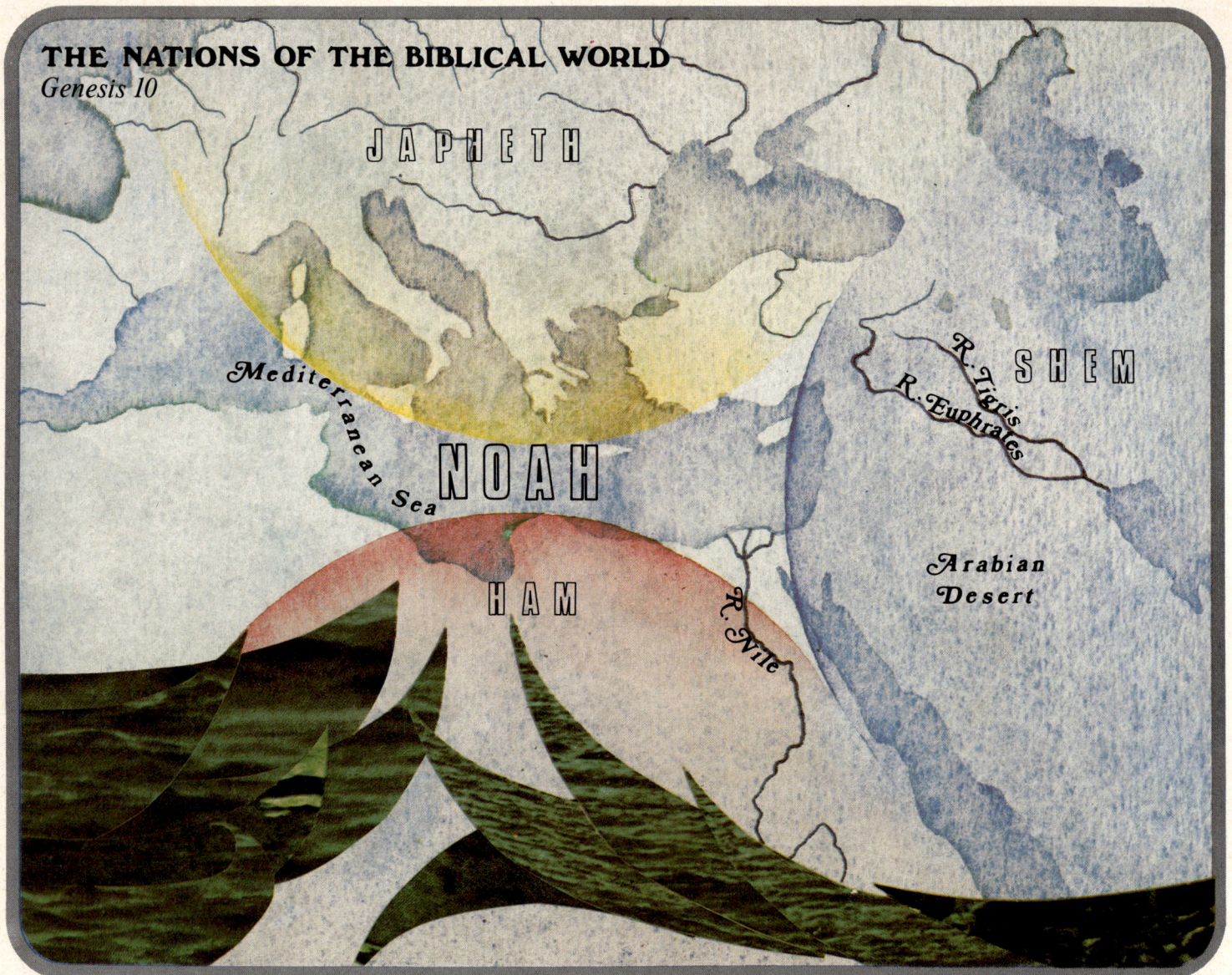

garden and enjoy its fruits. However, the fruit from the 'Tree of Knowledge' was forbidden, and Eve tempted Adam to eat from it: and because Adam and Eve had disobeyed God's command they were sent out of Eden. The story points out two important religious truths: firstly, that man has been given Free Will and so he is able to choose his own destiny, and secondly, the knowledge to distinguish between right and wrong. Mankind was meant to rise above animal behaviour and Godlessness and was to know the difference between good and evil. The action of Adam and Eve in eating the forbidden fruit needed an immediate answer from God for disobeying His commands. They had children but their family brought them suffering as well as joy.

Following this period we are told of a righteous man who "walked with God", Noah, and who lived at a time of great evil, violence and injustice. Because God could not tolerate this situation any longer, He asked Noah to build an Ark which would save him and his family from the Flood which was about to destroy the rest of mankind. People saw what Noah was building and he gave them the reason for it but they refused to listen to his warning and continued in their wicked ways. When the rains finally came, Noah, his wife, his three sons and their wives, together with pairs of every kind of living creature, boarded the Ark and stayed in it until the waters went down. The Flood proclaimed the eternal truth that human society must be based on

## CITY BUILDING AFTER THE FLOOD

*(map)*

Nineveh

*Mediterranean Sea*

MESOPOTAMIA

R. Tigris

R. Euphrates

SYRIA

Akkad

Babylon

LAND OF CANAAN

Ur

Via Maris

King

Zoan

On

EGYPT

*The Desert*

*Red Sea*

City
Main trade route
Cultivated land

justice, goodness and truth, without which mankind must perish. Noah's righteousness made him worthy of God's approval to establish a new era for humanity. Noah's sons, Ham, Shem and Japhet, became the ancestors of many nations.

Following the Flood, when people were still speaking one language, they planned to build a city in the plain of the land of Shinar near Babylon, in Mesopotamia, and also out of pride, a huge tower (Tower of Babel) that would reach to heaven. God frustrated their ambitions by confusing their language, thereby bringing a halt to their work.

The groups of people who descended from the three sons of Noah settled in areas where water was plentiful, such as the banks of the Nile river and the area around the two rivers Tigris and Euphrates. In the centre, bridging the two civilisations, lay the narrow strip of land by the Mediterranean Sea called the Land of Canaan, later to be known as the Holy Land. In three fertile areas the dawn of civilisation began, and the Book of Genesis describes in detail the ways and behaviour of the people living at that time. It speaks about the commercial activities and the various trades and occupations in which people were engaged, as well as the rivalry and wars between neighbouring countries and powers. In all these periods, the Land of the Bible is in the centre of the scene.

ABRAHAM'S JOURNEY TO CANAAN

Haran
Nineveh
MESOPOTAMIA
Great Sea
CANAAN
Jordan
EGYPT
Babylon
Arabian Desert
Ur
Fertile crescent

# THE PATRIARCHS AND THEIR WANDERINGS

*(Genesis 12 – Exodus 1)*
2,000-1,500 BCE

The history of the Jewish people begins with Abraham, the first of the three Patriarchs, who lived in the city of Ur on the River Euphrates, about 150 miles south-east of Babylon. Around the year 2,000 BCE Abraham saw how the civilisation in which he was living worshipped gods of wood and stone. However, he was convinced that there could only be one Creator who had created the world and who guided the lives of men with righteousness. The idea of an invisible God was, in those days, difficult to understand. It was at this stage that God made himself known to Abraham and said to him: "Leave your country, your family and your father's house, for the land I will show you. And I will make of you a great nation and I will bless you and make your name famous and you will be a blessing. And I shall bless those who bless you and those who curse you will themselves be cursed. And through you will all the families of the earth be blessed." Abraham followed God's instructions, left the city of Ur and travelled towards the land of Canaan, the Holy Land, accompanied by his wife Sarah and his nephew, Lot together with members of his household. Eventually they arrived at Shechem where God appeared to Abraham and said: "It is to your descendants that I will give this land". On the next stage of the journey, near Bethel, Abraham built an altar publicly announcing his belief and faith in God. At Mamre, near Hebron, he also built an altar to God, and it was in this same place that three angels came to visit Abraham to give him the news that an heir would be born to Sarah. It was here that he and his family became known as 'Hebrews', meaning people coming from 'the other side' of the Euphrates river. When Abraham and Sarah were both old God gave them a son, Isaac, as foretold by the angels, and whilst Isaac was still a boy God decided to test Abraham's faith as never before.

He commanded him to take Isaac to a far-off mountain and sacrifice him there. Without a murmur, Abraham obeyed, trusting in God's promise to his descendants, and bound Isaac onto the altar. As the knife was raised ready to kill, God's angel stopped Abraham from doing harm to Isaac. God saw that Abraham's faith was firm and He confirmed all the previous promises made to Abraham and his descendants who would be a cause of 'blessing to all the nations of the earth'. Abraham's belief and trust in God has made him an example for all time.

Sarah, the first of the four Matriarchs, died in Kiriath-arba, known as Hebron, and was buried in the cave of Machpelah which Abraham had bought from Ephron the son of Zohar. By this time Abraham was old and wanted to find a suitable wife for his son Isaac. So Eliezer, the chief servant of Abraham, was charged with the duty and was given certain descriptions of the type of girl that Isaac was to marry. She was to be good, kind, gentle, and of the same family background, so that God's promise of a great people descending from Abraham and his son Isaac would be fulfilled. In Haran, the city where Abraham had lived on his way to the Holy Land, lived his nephew. His daughter Rebekah had the right qualities, and Isaac loved her at sight.

Abraham died at the age 175, and was buried in the family grave which he had bought at Machpelah. Isaac followed in the way of his father trusting completely in God, although for the first 20 years of their marriage he and Rebekah had no children. But their prayers were answered when twin boys — Esau and Jacob — were born. They were entirely different in character, and Jacob became Rebekah's favourite whilst Esau was preferred by Isaac. Beersheba was to be the home of Isaac, who was a peace-loving person always anxious to avoid quarrels with neighbouring tribes, and Abimelech, the king of Gerar, concluded a peace treaty with Isaac recognising the fact that he was blessed with Divine guidance.

When Isaac became old and blind he asked Esau to bring him his favourite dish of venison. In order that Jacob should receive Isaac's blessing, Rebekah dressed him to appear like Esau, made a dish of food, and told Jacob to give it to his father. Isaac became suspicious when he heard Jacob's voice, but gave him his blessing.

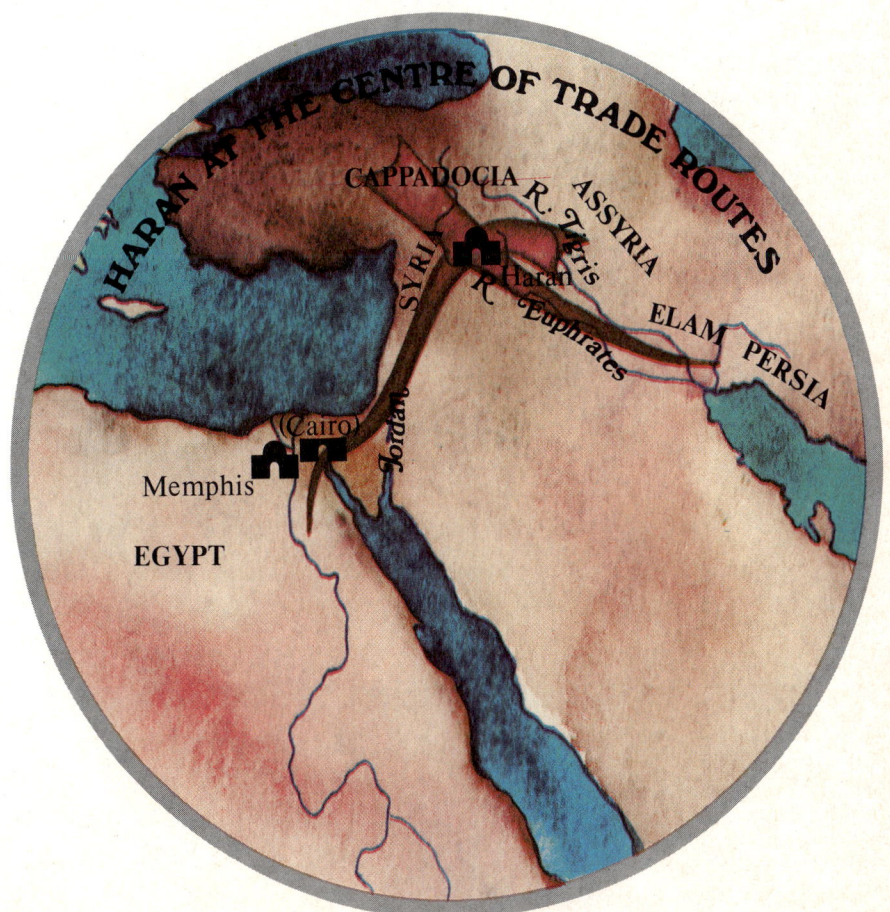

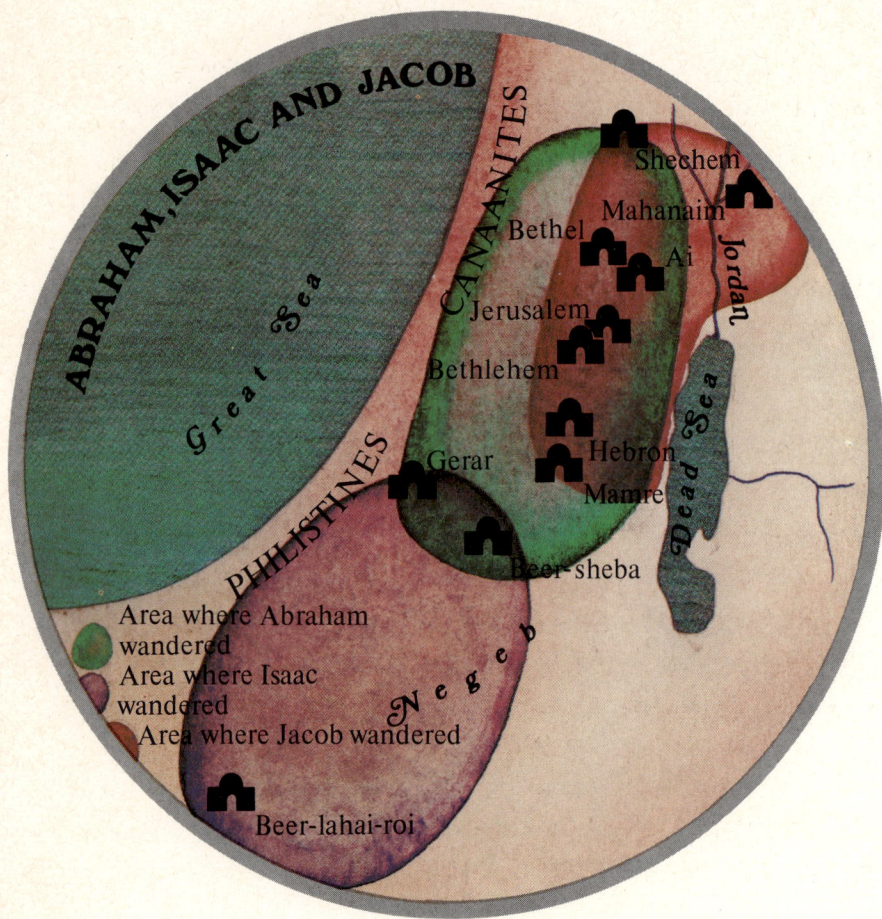

ABRAHAM, ISAAC AND JACOB

Great Sea

CANAANITES

PHILISTINES

Shechem

Mahanaim

Bethel

Ai

Jordan

Jerusalem

Bethlehem

Gerar

Hebron

Mamre

Dead Sea

Beer-sheba

Area where Abraham wandered

Area where Isaac wandered

Area where Jacob wandered

Negeb

Beer-lahai-roi

Soon Esau returned with the venison and the truth was discovered, but Esau pleaded with his father to bless him also, which Isaac did. However, Esau was so enraged that he vowed to kill his brother, and Jacob was forced to leave home. After getting Isaac's consent, Rebekah advised Jacob to go to her brother Laban in Haran. On his way from Beer-sheba, Jacob rested near the city of Luz, and dreamed of a staircase from Heaven to earth with angels ascending and descending on it. There also God appeared to him and repeated the promise made to his grandfather Abraham, that the ground on which he was resting would belong to his ancestors. To identify the place where he had had the vision, which was about 12 miles from Jerusalem, Jacob set up the stone on which he had slept, and called the place Bethel.

Jacob reached Laban's home and after working for him for a number of years married Laban's two daughters Leah and Rachel. Having worked hard, Jacob became a prosperous farmer and decided to return to his father's home in Hebron. By this time, Jacob had a large family and when he approached Edom, where his brother Esau had settled, he became fearful for their safety. Jacob sent a message of goodwill to his brother, but Esau gathered 400 men and went to meet Jacob. When Jacob was told of this, he divided his large group into two: so that if one group was attacked the other would be able to escape. Jacob prayed to God for deliverance and while he was alone an angel appeared and wrestled with him, but could not defeat him. Before he would release the angel, Jacob demanded his blessing. The request was granted and the angel also gave the new name 'Israel' (means: "He who strives with God") to Jacob, who called the place Penuel. When the brothers finally met, to Jacob's great relief, Esau gave him an affectionate and warm welcome: However, they then went their own ways after parting in peace. Jacob and his family stayed at Shechem for a considerable time and then continued their journey home. On the way he stopped at Bethel and built an altar to God for having spared him from the many dangers. On the journey, Jacob's beloved wife Rachel died whilst giving birth to her younger son, Benjamin. It was in Bethlehem that Jacob buried her and set up a memorial stone over her grave, which can be seen to this day. Jacob finally reached home in time to see his father before he died. Isaac lived 180 years, and he too was buried in the cave of Machpelah by his sons Esau and Jacob.

Hebron became once again the home for Jacob and his family. Joseph became his favourite child, and he made a 'coat of many colours' for him. This and Joseph's special dreams caused jealousy amongst his brothers who arranged to have him sold to a group of caravan travellers who were going to Egypt. There he was eventually made Pharaoh's Chief Minister and put in charge of preparations for a long famine. Joseph eventually saw his brothers again when they came to Egypt to buy corn during the famine. He revealed his identity to them and was at long last reunited with his father Jacob. Pharaoh allowed Jacob and his family to settle in Goshen, where they prospered and increased in numbers. When Jacob was approaching the end of his life he asked Joseph to promise that when he died he would be buried with his ancestors in the cave of Machpelah.

Joseph too, before he died made the Israelites take an oath that his remains would be taken with them when they eventually returned to the Holy Land.

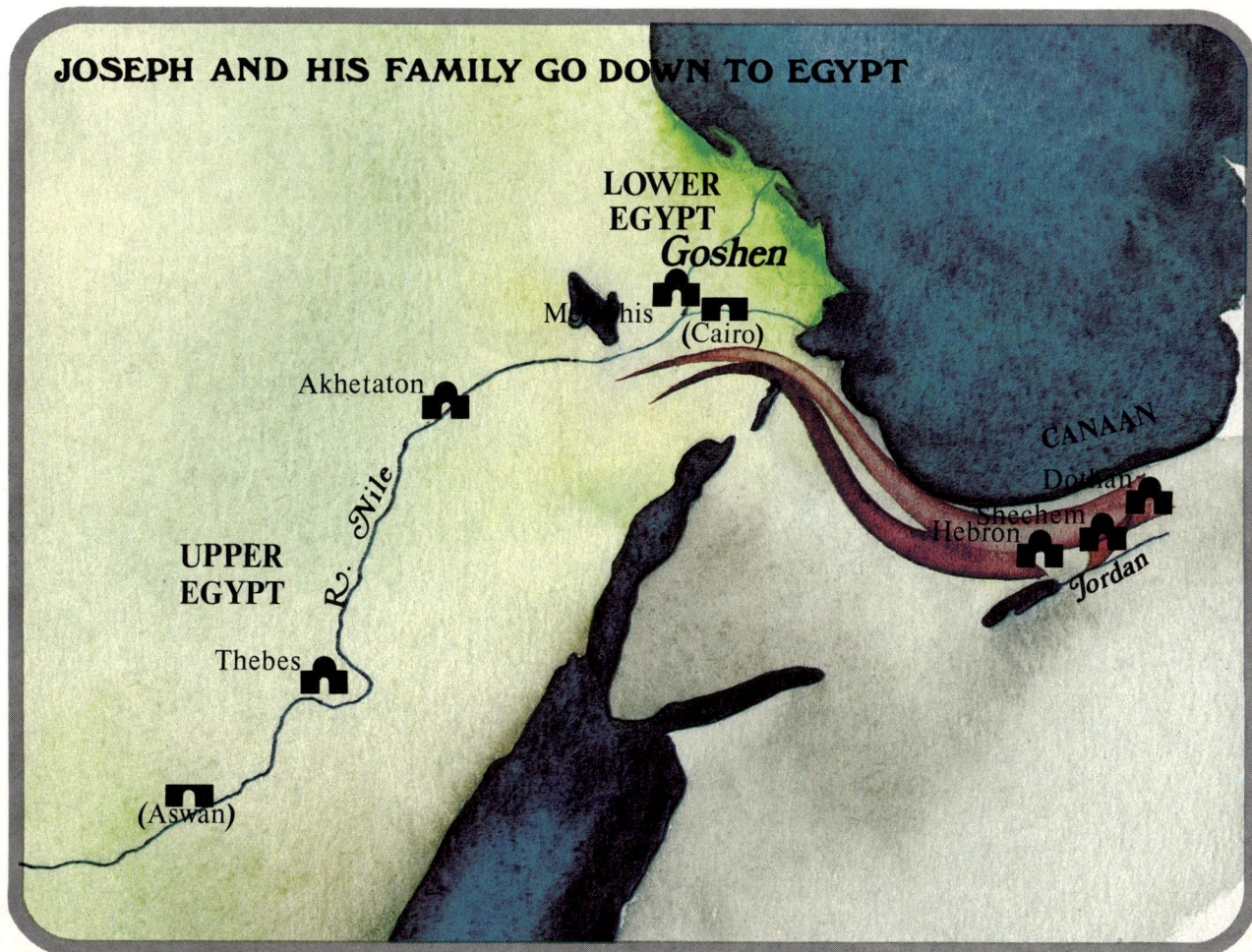

JOSEPH AND HIS FAMILY GO DOWN TO EGYPT

LOWER EGYPT
Goshen
Memphis
(Cairo)
Akhetaton
R. Nile
UPPER EGYPT
Thebes
(Aswan)
CANAAN
Dothan
Shechem
Hebron
Jordan

# MOSES AND THE EXODUS FROM EGYPT

*(Exodus 1-40)*

1,300 — 1,200 BCE

For a time the Israelites enjoyed the prosperity of their efforts and grew in numbers into a nation of almost two million people. In Egypt a Pharaoh, 'who did not know Joseph', feared the strength of the Hebrews, and forced them into slavery and made them build the stone-cities, Pithom and Rameses. They multiplied even more, however, so a command was given that all newborn Israelite boys be drowned in the River Nile. This order was disobeyed by the Hebrew midwives and despite all their suffering, the Israelites continued to increase in numbers. At this most critical time, the future leader of the Jewish people was born. Moses, who was brought up in the royal palace after he had been found in the reeds on the banks of the river by Pharaoh's daughter, was to lead his people from slavery to freedom. Moses never forgot his Hebrew origin and often went secretly to visit the Israelites working as slaves. He became angry at the cruel way in which the Israelites were treated by the Egyptians, and when he lost his temper and killed one of the overseers, he was forced to flee from Egypt and become a shepherd in the desert. There he was given a home by Jethro, the priest of Midian, and married Zipporah, one of Jethro's daughters.

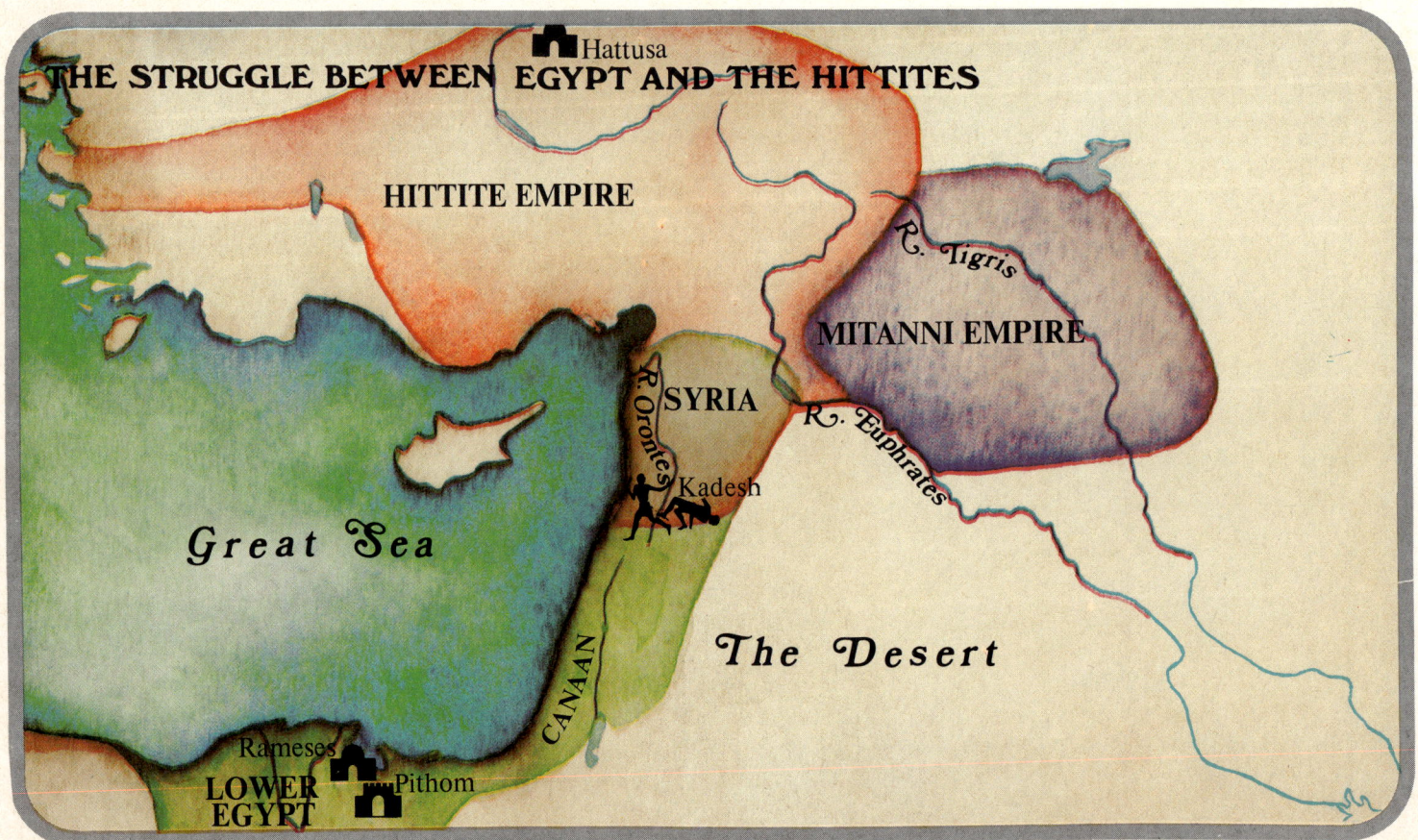

THE STRUGGLE BETWEEN EGYPT AND THE HITTITES

Hattusa

HITTITE EMPIRE

MITANNI EMPIRE

R. Tigris

R. Orontes

SYRIA

Kadesh

R. Euphrates

Great Sea

The Desert

CANAAN

Rameses

Pithom

LOWER EGYPT

One day, whilst looking after the sheep, Moses came across a bush which flamed but did not burn away. Surprised by such a sight he went closer to it and suddenly heard the voice of God speaking to him, commanding him to go back to Egypt and tell Pharaoh to let the Jewish people go. Confronted by Moses, Pharaoh refused, and it was only after the Egyptians had been afflicted by ten plagues that Pharaoh allowed Moses to lead the Israelites out of Egypt. Soon after they had left Egypt, Pharaoh changed his mind and pursued the Israelites, who by that time had reached the Red Sea. At God's command the Israelites crossed the sea on dry land with the waters forming a wall on either side, and escaped into the desert. When Pharaoh and his army followed they were engulfed by the waters of the sea which resumed its normal course.

Then began the wanderings in the Wilderness of Shur and Etham by the banks of the Red Sea going towards Rephidim in the Wilderness of Sin. It was in Rephidim that the Amalekites decided to fight the Israelites, who in turn fought back, led by Joshua. At sunset, Amalek was defeated and God told Moses to write down this treacherous act of the Amalekites which was never to be forgotten.

Three months after the Israelites had left Egypt they reached the Wilderness of Sinai. It was here that Moses the leader went to the top of Mount Sinai whilst every man, woman and child gathered around the foot of the mountain. God gave Moses the two tablets of stone on which were engaved the Ten Commandments which God had proclaimed and which had been heard by all the Israelites. Moses remained on top of the mount for forty days to receive further commandments.

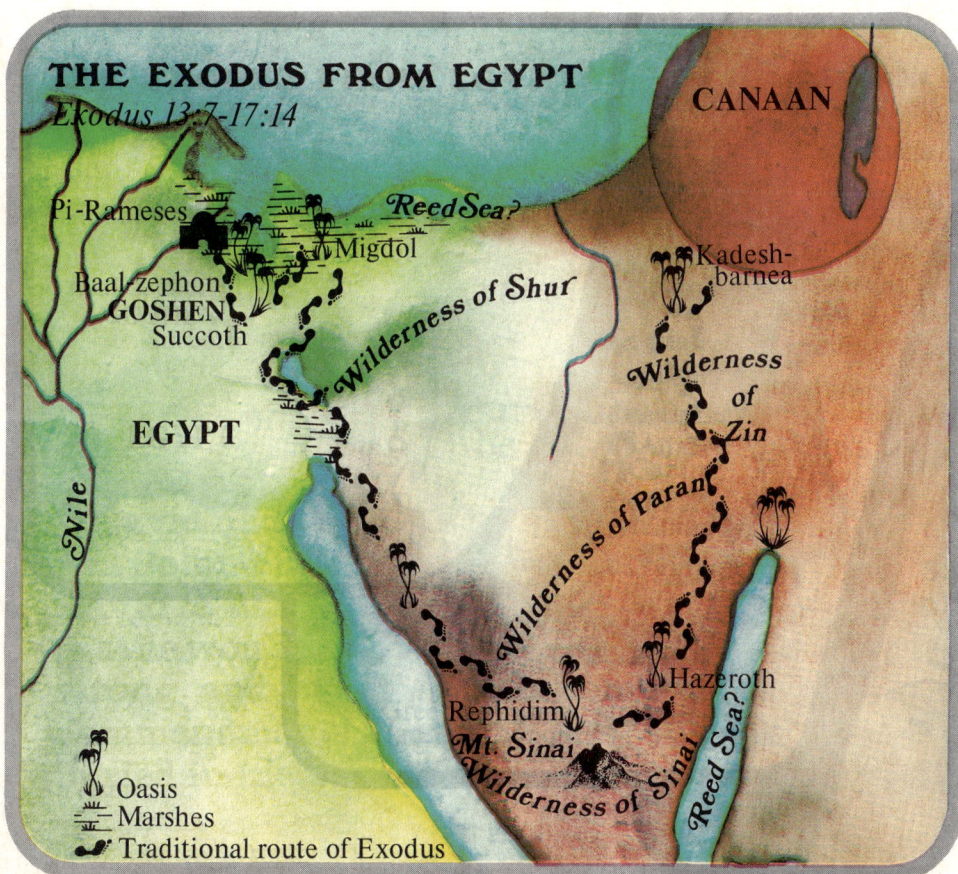

THE EXODUS FROM EGYPT
Exodus 13:7-17:14

CANAAN

Pi-Rameses
Reed Sea?
Migdol
Baal-zephon
GOSHEN
Succoth
Wilderness of Shur
Kadesh-barnea
Wilderness of Zin
EGYPT
Wilderness of Paran
Nile
Hazeroth
Rephidim
Mt. Sinai
Wilderness of Sinai
Reed Sea?

Oasis
Marshes
Traditional route of Exodus

## CANAANITE PERIOD

### c.3000 BCE
Beginning of recorded history of the area. Semi-desert region, nomadic tribes, city states, fortified towns.

### c.2000-1500 BCE
Age of the Patriarchs.

### c.1300 BCE
Exodus from Egypt.

In the meantime the people became rather impatient thinking that Moses would never return. They asked Aaron, the brother of Moses, to create an object which they could see and worship and be their visible leader. Aaron, hoping that his brother would in the meantime come down from the mountain, told the people to bring golden objects out of which he would form a calf. When it was completed, the people began to worship the new idol, bringing it sacrifices and singing and dancing.

This angered God and He told Moses to go down to the people immediately. As Moses approached the foot of the mountain he heard the sound of singing and dancing and when he saw the Golden Calf, he was so enraged that he threw the tablets of stone containing the Ten Commandments to the ground and destroyed the calf. The tribe of Levi, who were not involved in the act of idolatry, were commanded to punish the ringleaders.

Moses pleaded with God to forgive the Israelites for all that they had done. God pardoned their sin and told Moses to return to the top of Mount Sinai. There he stayed for another forty days during which time he neither ate nor drank. At the end of this period Moses returned to the people carrying another pair of tablets of stone inscribed with the Ten Commandments. He then communicated the Torah, all the laws which he had received from

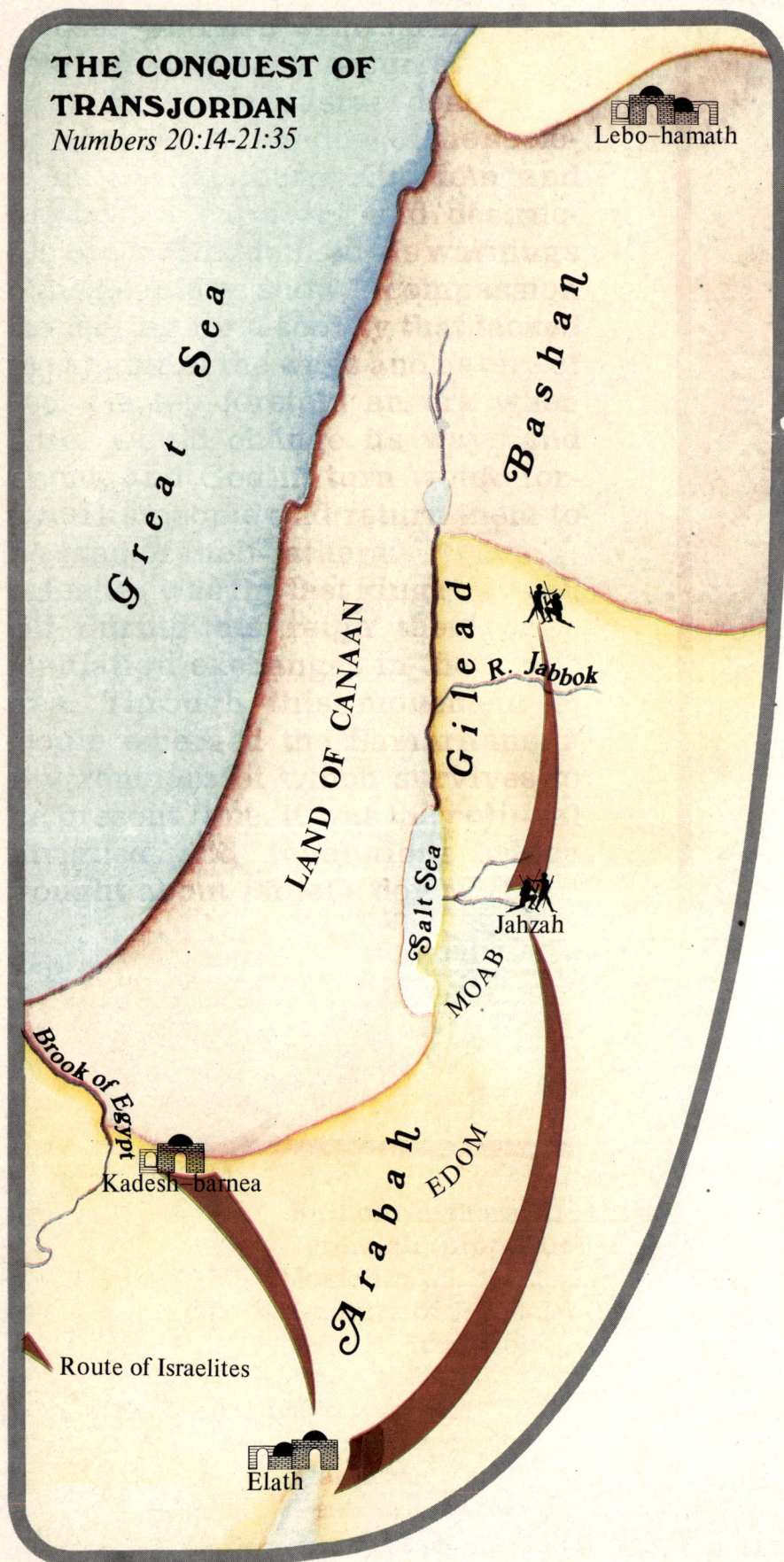

## THE CONQUEST OF TRANSJORDAN
*Numbers 20:14-21:35*

Lebo-hamath

Great Sea

Bashan

Gilead

R. Jabbok

LAND OF CANAAN

Salt Sea

Jahzah

MOAB

Brook of Egypt

Kadesh-barnea

Arabah

EDOM

Route of Israelites

Elath

God, to Aaron, the elders and all the Israelites, who declared with one voice, "All that the Lord has spoken, we shall do". Soon after this event, Moses the lawgiver instructed the people to build the Sanctuary which was to be used all the time they were travelling towards the Promised Land.

The Priests and the Levites were chosen to serve in the Sanctuary which consisted of an outer court, the Tabernacle and the Holy of Holies into which the High Priest alone entered only once a year on the Day of Atonement. When the Sanctuary was completed, ceremonies lasting seven days took place. Moses who had supervised its building blessed the people for the way they had carried out their holy work.

| | |
|---|---|
| Abraham ........... | c.1900 BCE |
| Isaac .................... | c.1800 BCE |
| Jacob ................. | c.1750 BCE |
| Joseph ............... | c.1700 BCE |
| Joseph in Egypt | c.1650 BCE |
| Exodus from Egypt | 1230 BCE |

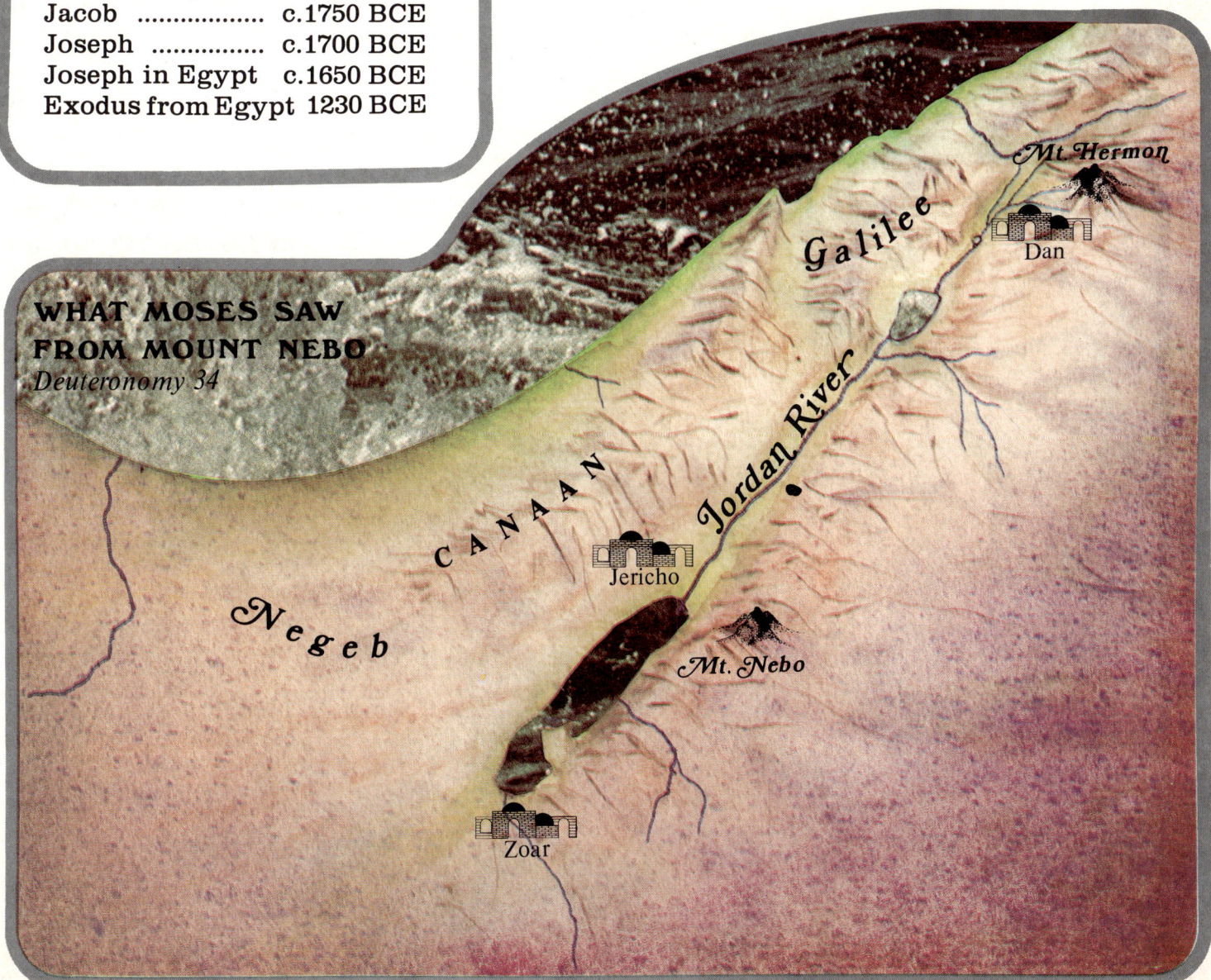

**WHAT MOSES SAW FROM MOUNT NEBO**
*Deuteronomy 34*

Mt. Hermon

Galilee

Dan

Jordan River

CANAAN

Jericho

Negeb

Mt. Nebo

Zoar

# JOSHUA AND THE CONQUEST OF CANAAN

*(Joshua 1-24; Judges 1-2)*

c. 1,200 BCE

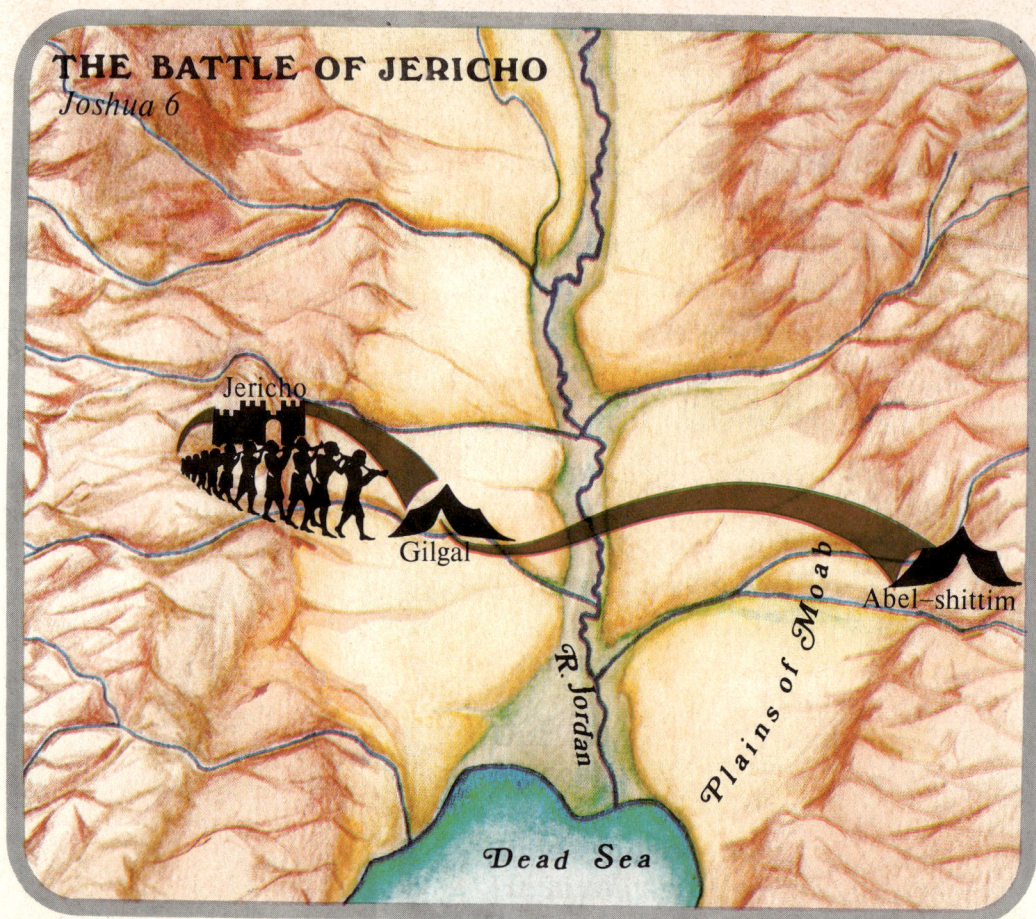

**THE BATTLE OF JERICHO**
*Joshua 6*

It was Joshua's responsibility to prepare a campaign which would result in the Israelites inhabiting the Holy Land. He was inspired by God's blessing of "be strong and of good courage". In order to test the strength of the fortified city of Jericho, which commanded a key position in the area, Joshua sent two spies who returned with a report that the people living in Jericho were much afraid of an invasion by the Israelites. On God's instructions, priests marched round the walls of Jericho once a day for six days, and on the seventh day seven circuits were made followed by a long blast by the trumpets. The Israelites gave a mighty shout and the walls collapsed. They then burned the city and the victory made the way clear for the Israelites to enter the centre of Canaan. Recent discoveries support the Biblical account of how Jericho fell.

The people were now on the other side of the River Jordan and Moses had previously ordered the Israelites to observe a ceremony at Mounts Ebal and Gerizim before the conquest of the Holy Land. Six of the tribes stood on Mount Gerizim, the side representing 'the blessed' and the other six stood on Mount Ebal, representing 'the cursed'. The Levites who were in the valley between the mounts pronounced the 'blessings' which the people would enjoy if they listened to the word of God, and the 'curses' and punishments if they would disobey God's commandments. To this very day Mount Ebal is bare and scorched earth and Mount Gerizim is full of vegetation and wooded areas. During all the forty years of wandering in the Wilderness the Israelites carried with them the remains of Joseph and when they arrived at the city of Shechem, near Mount Gerizim, they buried him there.

The tribes of Reuben and Gad possessed large herds of cattle which needed rich pasture and plenty of water, so they were given the land on the east side of the Jordan river. Part of the tribe of Manasseh too was allowed to settle in this area. But first the men had to help conquer the rest of the Holy Land and make sure that the other tribes were settled in the allotted region. With God's help, Joshua guided the Israelites until the whole of Canaan was conquered. There were many battles which were not easily won and many obstacles came in the way of ultimate victory. One of these instances was when the people of Gibeon heard that the Israelites were approaching and they knew that they would be powerless in the face of Joshua, so they tried to make peace with him. In the meantime, the neighbouring five kings of the Amorite cities became hostile towards Gibeon and made war against the inhabitants of Gibeon. They pleaded with Joshua to save them from the Amorites. Joshua summoned his soldiers, travelled all night, caught the Amorite kings unawares and fought a great battle and defeated them. The battle continued all day long and night was about to fall when he prayed to God that He should "cause the sun to stand still over Gibeon and let the moon remain stationary" so that he could complete the military operation and let none escape. Miraculously, the sun stood still and did not set the whole day, and Joshua was able to bring the battle to a victorious end.

From then on the Israelites went from victory to victory. Their faith in God gave them added courage and strength. By this time Joshua was growing old, and at Gilgal supervised and decided on the division of the Holy Land for the other nine and a half tribes. This was done by the casting of lots and territories were set aside for the second part of the

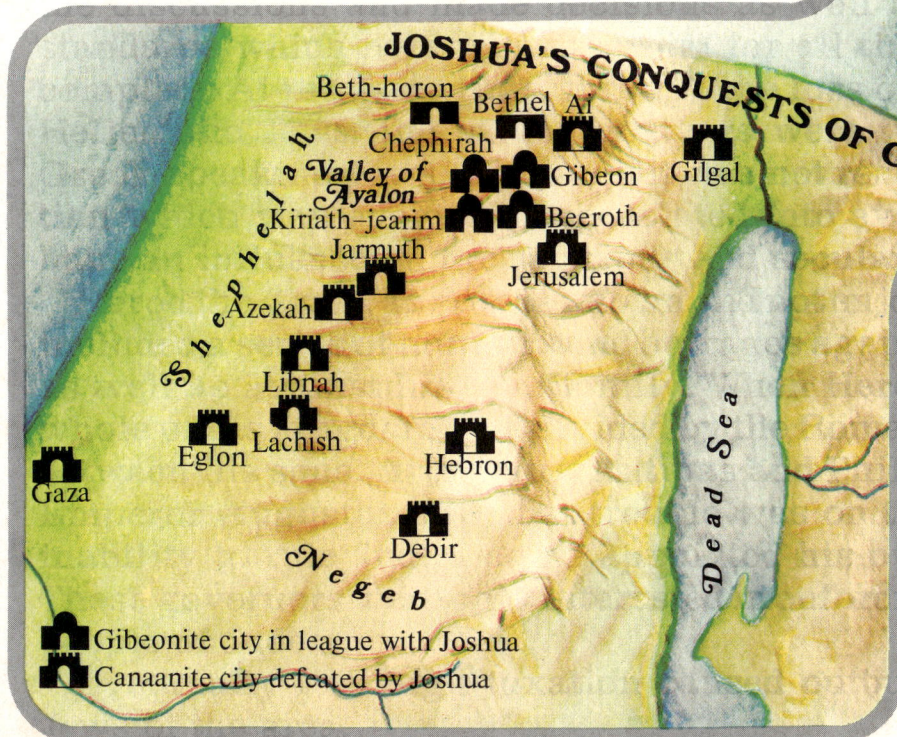

tribe of Manasseh, Judah and Ephraim. At a later stage, when Joshua set up the Tabernacle at Shiloh the remaining seven tribes were allotted their particular area of land (see map on page 22).

No separate territory was given to the tribe of Levi who had special tasks such as ministering in the sanctuary

JOSHUA'S CONQUESTS OF CANAAN

Misrephot-maim
Madon (Merom)
Hazor
Sea of Chinnereth
Achshaph
Shimron
Plain of Jezreel
Beth-horon
Bethel Ai
Chephirah
Valley of Ayalon
Gibeon
Gilgal
Kiriath-jearim
Beeroth
Jarmuth
Jerusalem
Azekah
Shephelah
Libnah
Lachish
Eglon
Hebron
Gaza
Dead Sea
Debir
Negeb

Gibeonite city in league with Joshua
Canaanite city defeated by Joshua

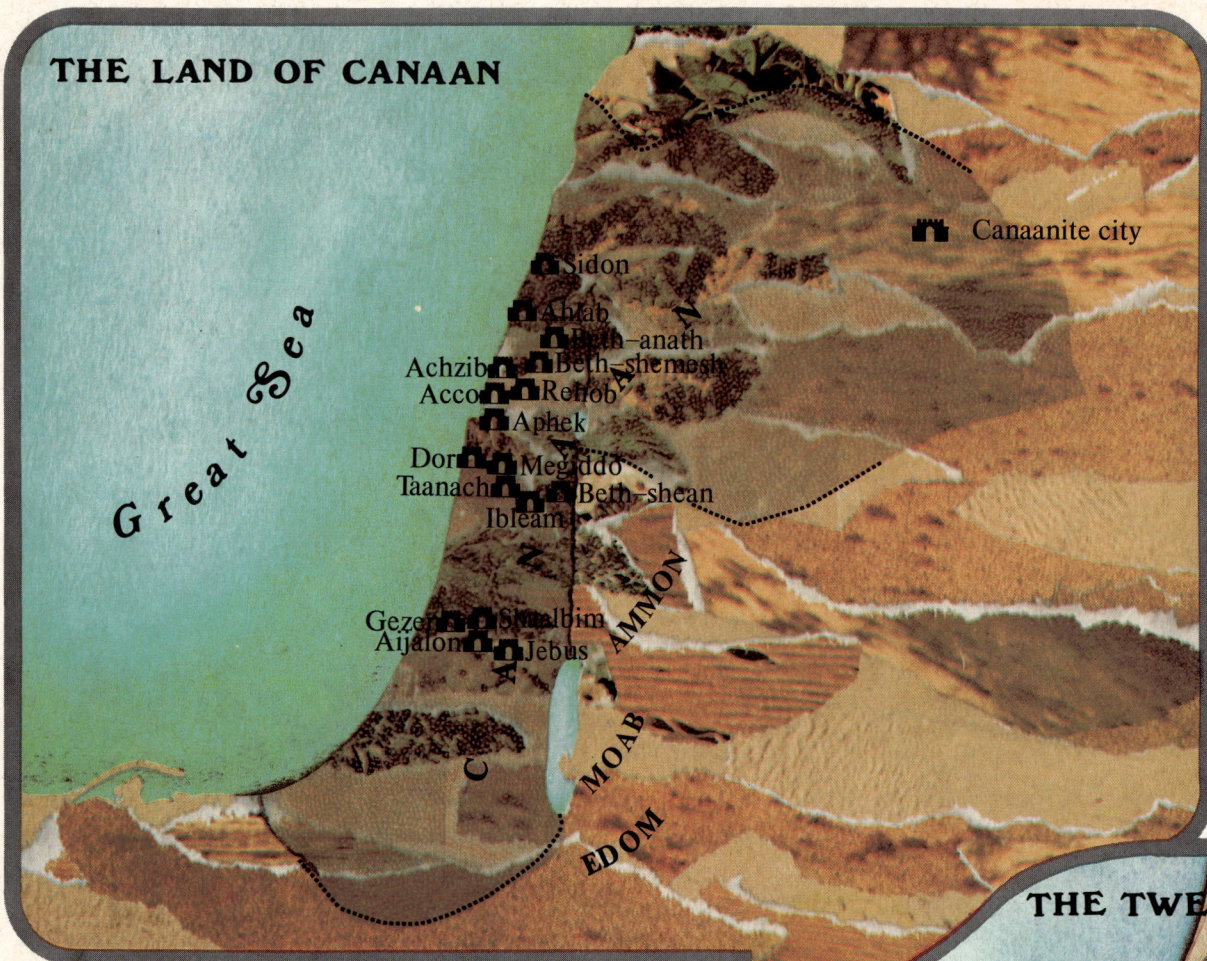

## THE LAND OF CANAAN

🏰 Canaanite city

Sidon
Ahlab
Beth-anath
Achzib  Beth-shemesh
Acco  Rehob
Aphek
Dor  Megiddo
Taanach  Beth-shean
Ibleam

Gezer  Shaalbim
Aijalon  Jebus

AMMON
MOAB
EDOM

*Great Sea*

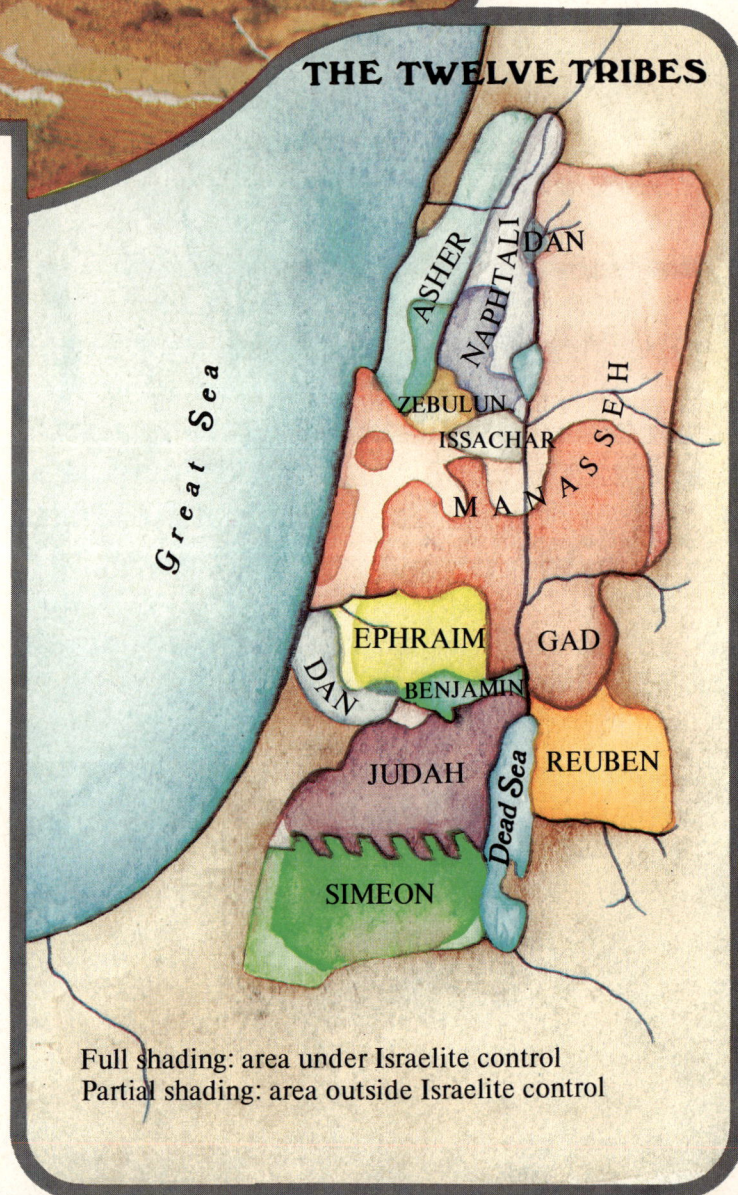

## THE TWELVE TRIBES

ASHER  NAPHTALI  DAN
ZEBULUN
ISSACHAR
MANASSEH
EPHRAIM  GAD
BENJAMIN
DAN
JUDAH  REUBEN
SIMEON

*Great Sea*
*Dead Sea*

Full shading: area under Israelite control
Partial shading: area outside Israelite control

and acting as teachers and welfare officers to the people. They were to receive 48 cities on both sides of the river Jordan for their maintenance. Also there was no tribe of Joseph as such, but the descendants of his sons, Ephraim and Manasseh were to be included in the division of the land.

Joshua was pleased that at long last the Israelites were resting from wars and would be able to possess and dwell in the land which God had promised them. When he was about to die, Joshua addressed the leaders and the people at Shechem, reminding them of their past history and of their future role as a 'Kingdom of priests and a holy nation'. He told them that God had fulfilled his promise and now they must observe His teachings and laws as given to them by Moses their teacher.

The people answered by saying that they would be loyal and serve

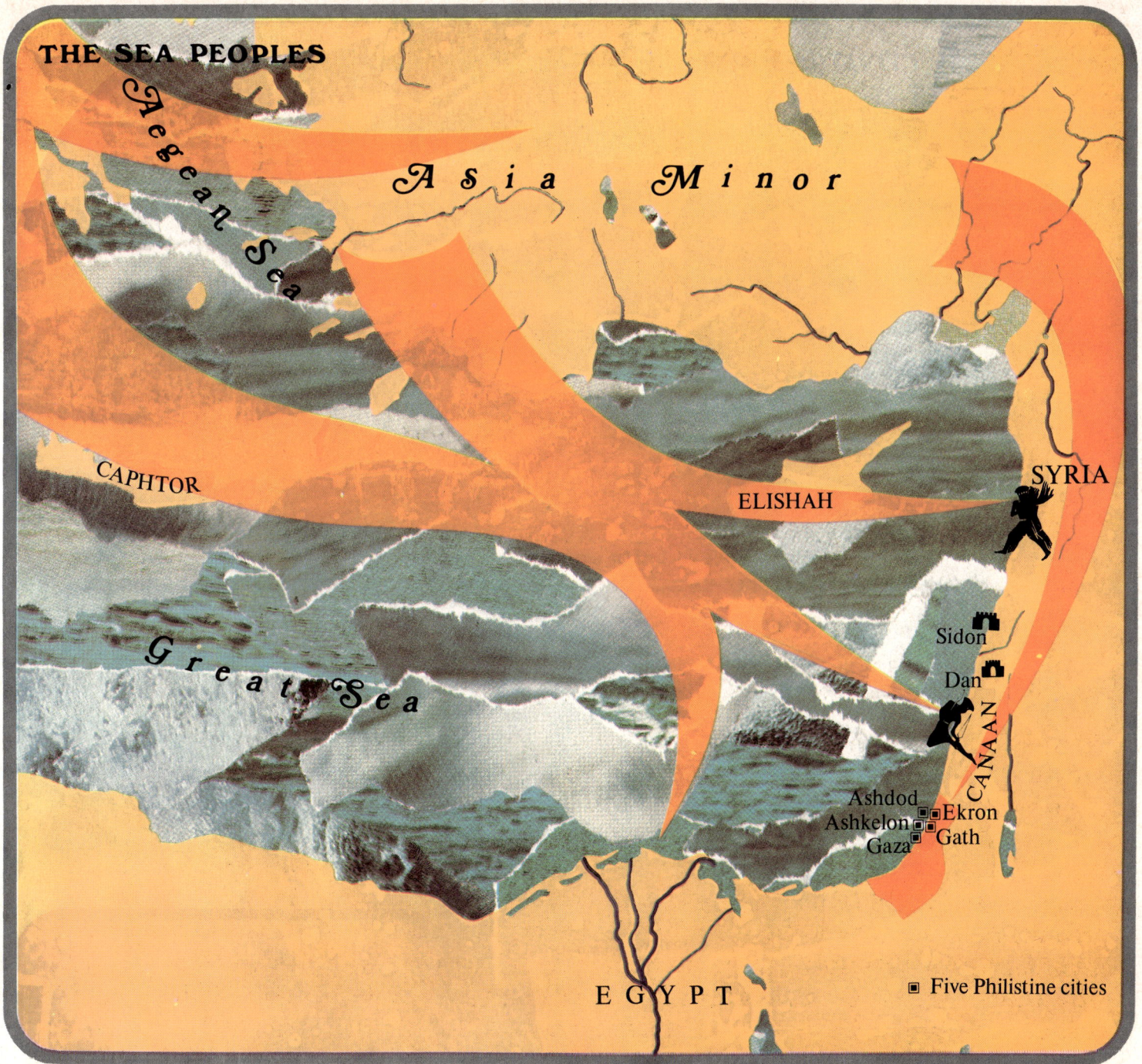

## THE SEA PEOPLES

Aegean Sea

Asia Minor

CAPHTOR

ELISHAH

SYRIA

Great Sea

Sidon

Dan

CANAAN

Ashdod
Ashkelon — Ekron
Gaza — Gath

EGYPT

■ Five Philistine cities

God forever. Joshua died in peace at the age of 110, knowing that the Israelites would listen to God's voice, and he was buried in his own territory of Ephraim near the city of Shechem.

| | |
|---|---|
| Settlement in the Holy Land | 1500 BCE |
| Deborah | 1150 BCE |
| Samson | 1100 BCE |
| Saul | 1028-1003 BCE |
| David | 1013-973 BCE |
| Solomon | 973-933 BCE |

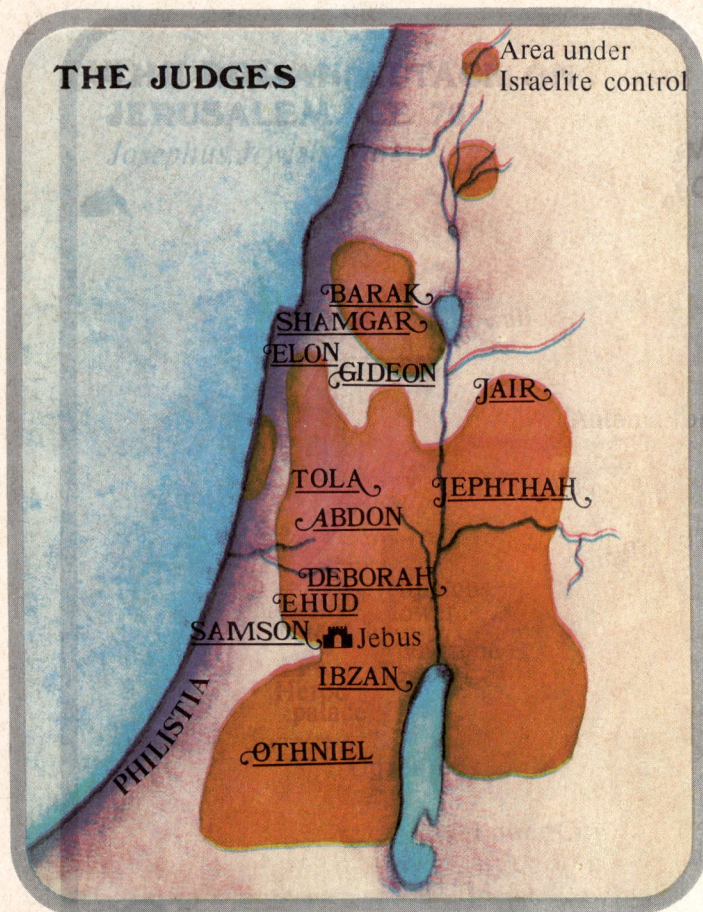

**THE JUDGES**

Area under Israelite control

BARAK
SHAMGAR
ELON
GIDEON
JAIR
TOLA
JEPHTHAH
ABDON
DEBORAH
EHUD
SAMSON Jebus
IBZAN
OTHNIEL
PHILISTIA

# THE DAYS OF THE JUDGES

*(Judges 1-21; Samuel 1-8)*

1,200 — 1,025 BCE

For a time the Tribes of Israel knew of no trouble or distress. The Elders and Priests who were their leaders remembered Moses and Joshua and their teachings. These were followed by Judges who were also the leaders of the people, and it was about this time, around the 11th century BCE, that the Israelites began to forget the warnings of Moses and Joshua and disobeyed the commandments of God. It was the task of the Judge at the time to give inspiration, and courage and finally to rescue the Israelites from the invaders who were surrounding them. They included the Moabites, the Canaanites, the Midianites, the Ammonites and the Philistines.

It was Ehud from the tribe of Benjamin who gathered around him soldiers who expelled the Moabites from the territory of Benjamin after they had invaded the area and oppressed the people for 18 years. In the north of the country the northern Canaanites oppressed the Israelites for 20 years and it was Deborah, the prophetess and judge, who lived in the hills of Ephraim, who was determined to end the misery of the Israelites in this area where Jabin, King of Canaan, had reduced the status of the people to that of slaves. She ordered Barak of the tribe of Naphtali to form an army and eventually defeated the Canaanite oppressors, including their captain Sisera, who was slain by Jael in whose tent he had sheltered.

The Midianites were the next invaders and overran the Holy Land as far west as Gaza. The Israelites, out of fear, left their homes and lived in caves, strongholds and dens. For seven years the people were oppressed when Gideon, who lived in a city of Manasseh, had a vision in which an angel told him that God had chosen him to deliver the Israelites from their oppressors. Gideon gathered around him 32,000 warriors but this number was consider-

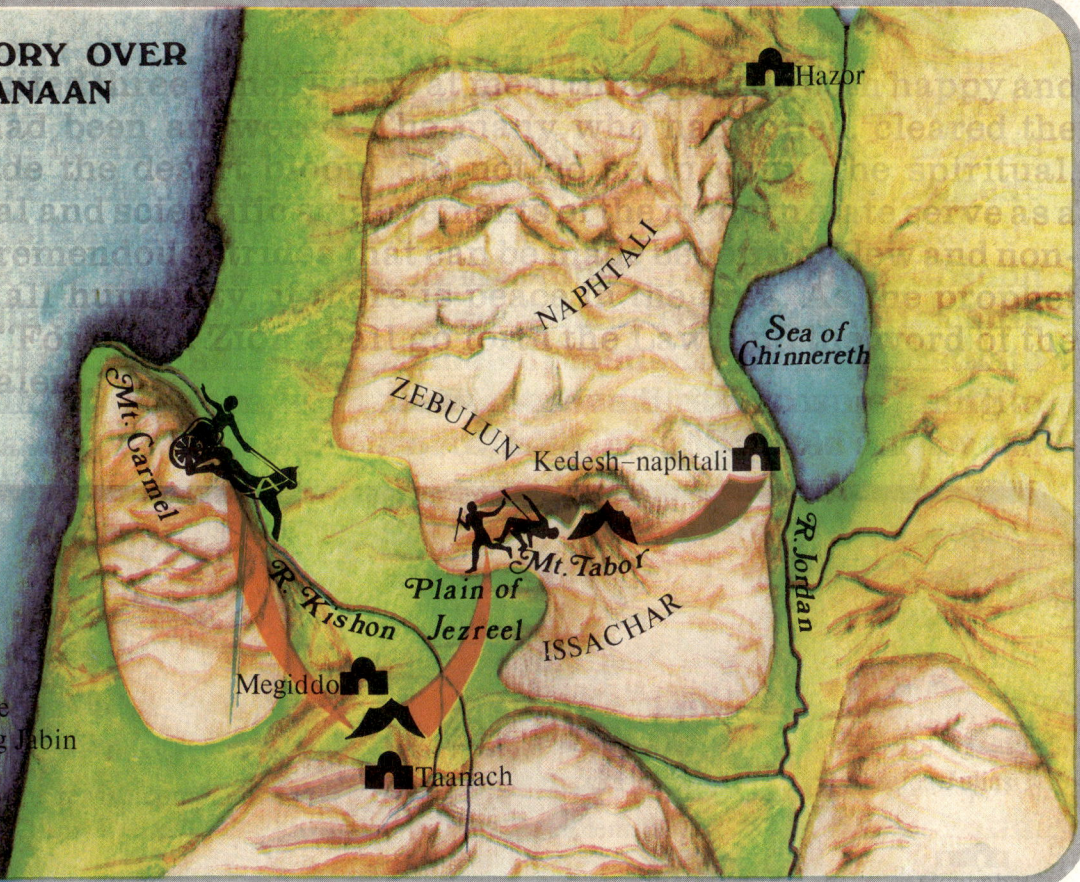

**DEBORAH'S VICTORY OVER JABIN, KING OF CANAAN**
*Judges 4,5*

Hazor

Sea of Chinnereth

NAPHTALI

ZEBULUN

Kedesh–naphtali

Mt. Carmel

R. Kishon

Mt. Tabor

Plain of Jezreel

ISSACHAR

R. Jordan

Megiddo

Thanach

Israelite force
Canaanite chariot force
Canaanites under King Jabin
Israelites

ably reduced as all those who feared battle were dismissed and told to return to their homes. God told Gideon that even with the 10,000 who remained there were still too many for the battle against the Midianites as the people would believe that it was because of their might and numbers that the Israelites were victorious. Other tests were made to find the bravest soldiers of all Israel, then only 300 men remained to fight the battle, which resulted in the entire Midianite army running away in fear and terror.

However, soon after these events the Israelites forgot God and his teachings and sinned. As on the previous occasions, the punishment for their misdeeds took the form of oppression by a neighbouring nation, the Ammonites, who persecuted and oppressed the Israelites for 18 years, especially in the district of Gilead. A person who had the right qualities for leadership, called Jephtah, was persuaded to lead the Israelites in battle against the Ammonites. He gathered his forces together at Mizpah and made a thoughtless promise which caused his only daughter to be killed on his successful return from the battle. For six years Jephtah was a Judge over the Israelites.

Another neighbour hostile to the Israelites were the Philistines who lived near the Mediterranean sea. For 40 years they harassed the people living in the Holy Land and particularly those who were in the area settled by the tribe of Dan. At that time a great warrior and hero appeared who lived near the coast close to where Tel Aviv is today. His parents had a vision when they were told that their child would deliver Israel from the Philistines. This boy, Samson, was brought up as a Nazarite, drinking no wine or strong drink and never cutting his hair. As he grew into manhood it was found that he had extraordinary strength and great courage. Many interesting and exciting adventures were recorded about him.

Samson, whilst on his way to Timnah, was pounced on by a young lion and with his bare hands tore the lion apart. Another time Samson was staying in Gaza and his enemies quickly closed the gates of the city waiting for the morning to kill him. But when midnight came, and the people of the city were asleep, he unhinged the two huge and heavy gates and carried them on his shoulders to the top of a hill near Hermon. His courage and strength made him famous with the Israelites for over 20 years. It was when he fell in love with Delilah, who found out that the secret of his strength lay in his uncut hair, that Samson drew near to his death. While he was asleep, Delilah, who had been bribed by the Philistine chieftains, ordered his hair to be cut off, after which the Philistines seized him, blinded him and bound him in chains. Then he was put into prison, but as his hair grew again he regained his strength. At a Philistine festivity in their temple of Dagon, Samson was brought in so that they could make fun of him. He asked to be led to the two main pillars and prayed to God for strength. Samson pushed the pillars apart and the whole temple collapsed killing all who were present, including Samson himself. His body was rescued and buried in the territory of Dan.

During the days of the Judges there was a famine in the Land of Judah, and Elimelech together with his wife Naomi and his two sons left Bethlehem to go to Moab where more food was available. The Moabites were descended from Abraham's nephew, Lot, and they treated the refugee family kindly, allow-

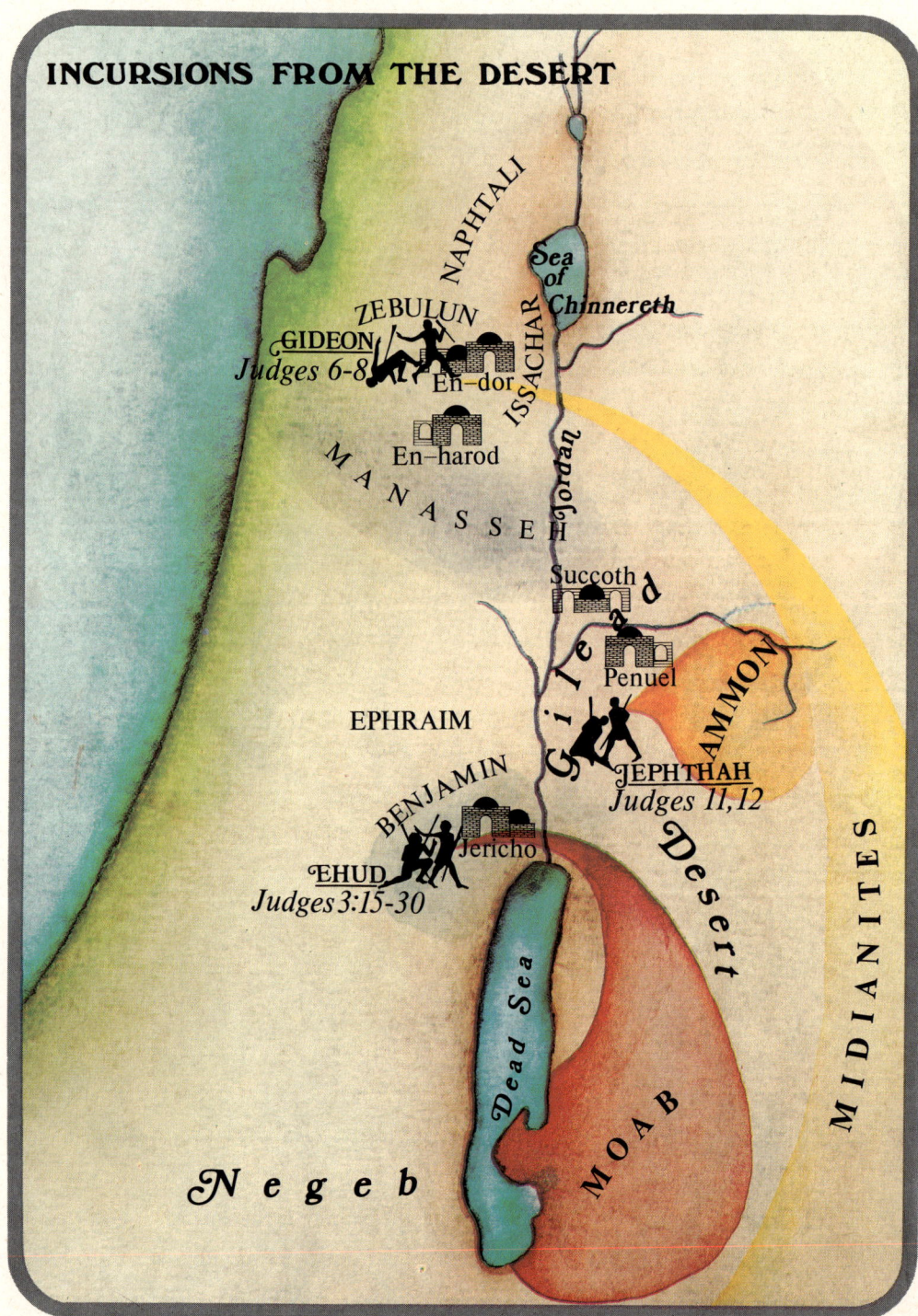

INCURSIONS FROM THE DESERT

R.Sorek

Gezer

Timnah

Ekron   Zorah

Ashdod   Gath

Ashkelon

Shephelah

Dead Sea

Gaza

PHILISTIA

JUDAH

Brook of Egypt

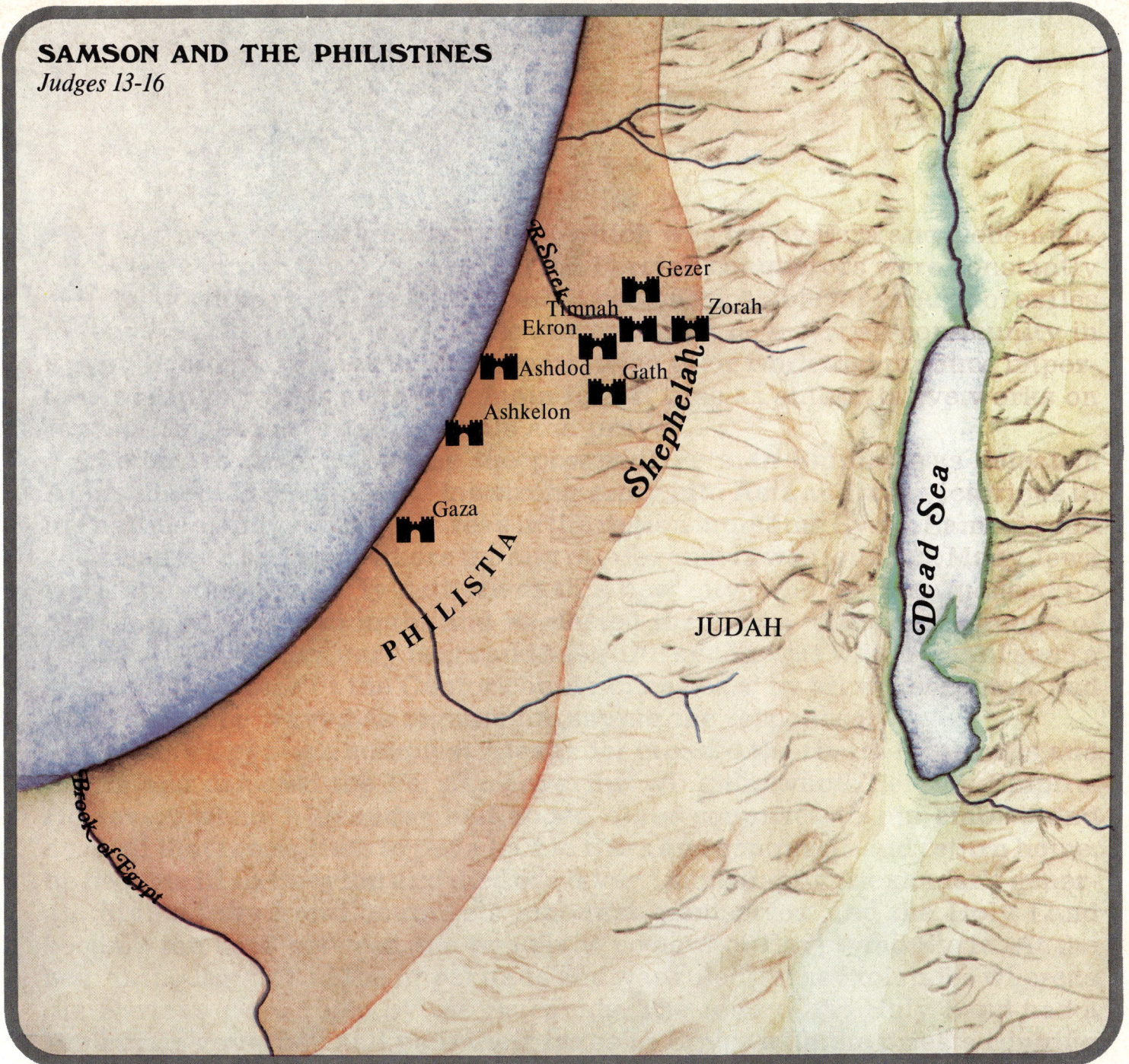

ing them to till the land and so by hard work they made a living. In the meantime, the two sons of Elimelech married two Moabite girls and a little later the death of Elimelech was followed by the death of both sons. This caused Naomi to be left with her two daughters-in-law, Orpah and Ruth.

Meanwhile the famine had ended and Naomi decided to return to Bethlehem. Orpah decided to remain in Moab after Naomi tried to persuade both women to go back to their parents and begin new lives, but Ruth insisted on going with Naomi back to Bethlehem and remain with her and fully accept her way of life and beliefs.

Eventually Ruth married Boaz who was a relative of Elimelech and they had a son named Obed whose grandson was David, who became King over all Israel.

Soon after Samson died, the Philistines began a military attack against the Israelites at Shiloh, which was the religious centre of the whole country and the place where the Tabernacle had stood since the days of Joshua. For over 40 years Eli the High Priest and Judge served the people, and he took under his care a young boy called Samuel, whose mother had promised to dedicate his life to God's service. When Samuel grew up he influenced the people to be united and defeat the Philistines. At Mizpah he held a day of prayer following which the Israelites gained complete victory and recaptured the many cities which they had lost previously.

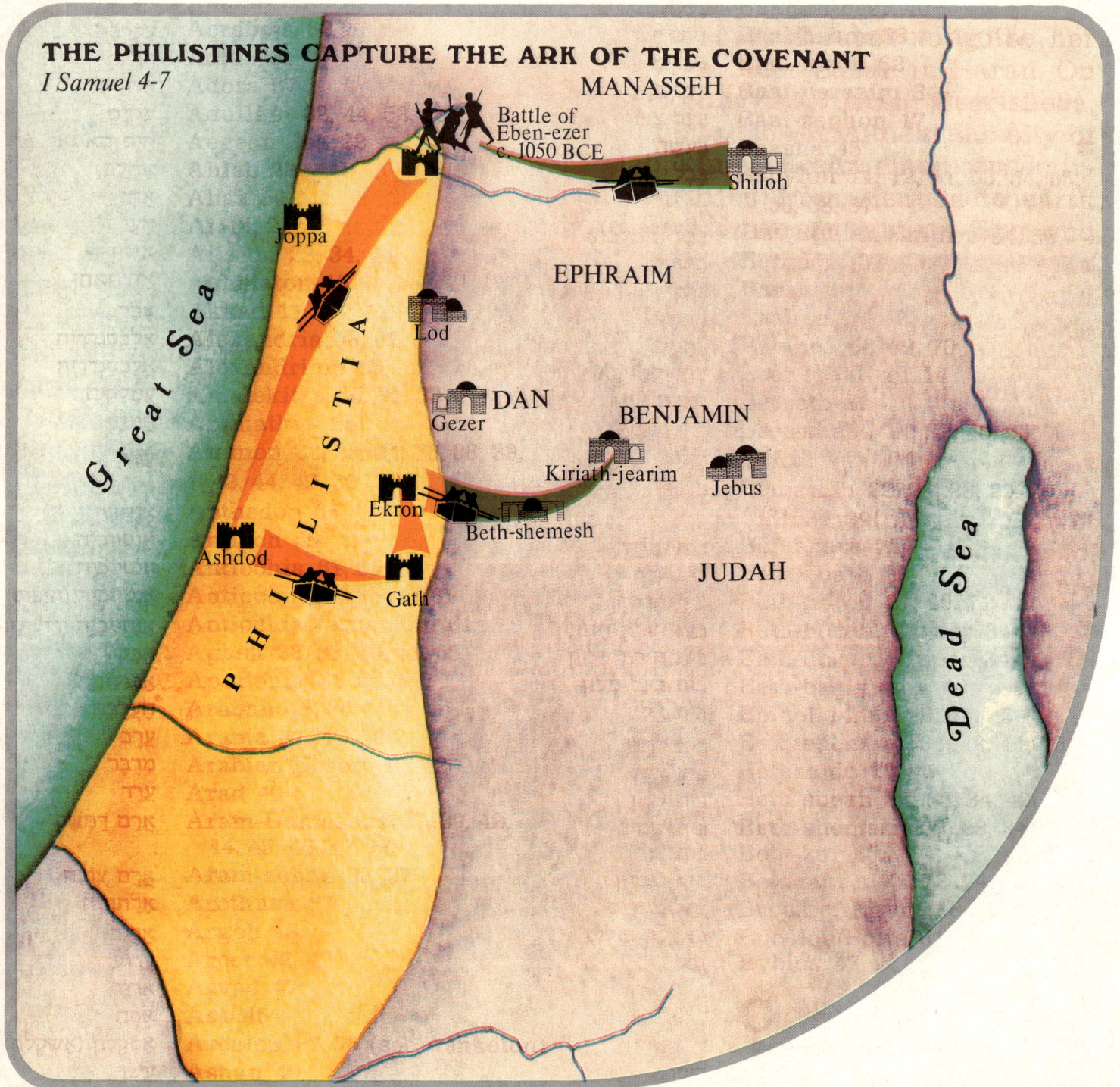

**THE PHILISTINES CAPTURE THE ARK OF THE COVENANT**
*I Samuel 4-7*

MANASSEH

Battle of
Eben-ezer
c. 1050 BCE

Shiloh

Joppa

EPHRAIM

Great Sea

Lod

DAN

Gezer

BENJAMIN

Kiriath-jearim

Jebus

Ekron

Beth-shemesh

PHILISTIA

Ashdod

JUDAH

Gath

Dead Sea

When the prophet Samuel became old, the Israelites decided that they wanted to have a king as their leader. The elders approached Samuel with their request and he prayed for guidance concerning this important matter. God told Samuel to listen to the voice of the elders and to choose a king. It was to be Saul, who lived in Gibeah, who was to be the first King of Israel. Saul had an imposing appearance, being taller than most men, and having handsome features which impressed the people and filled them with admiration. He was acclaimed as their King and leader.

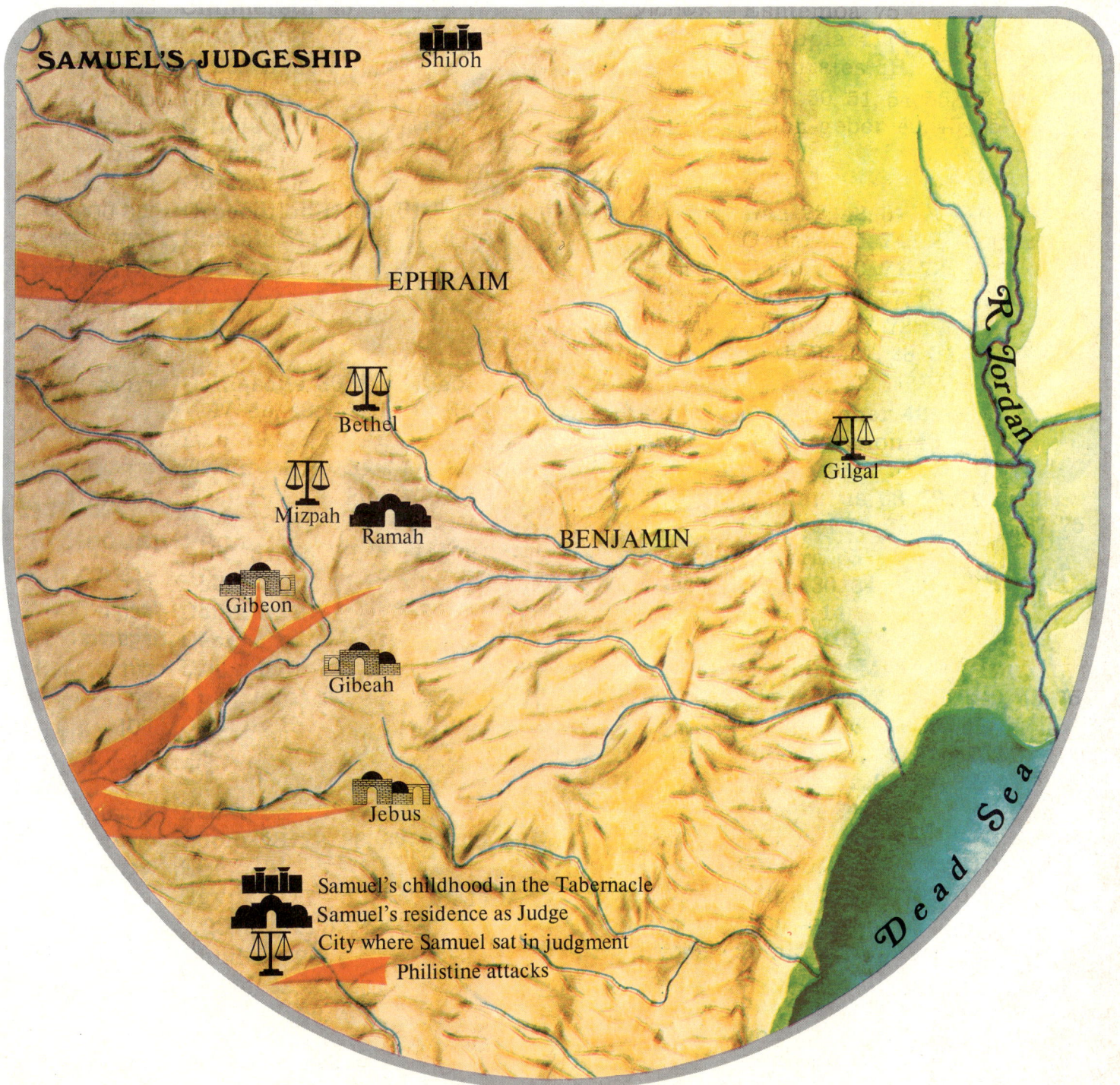

**SAMUEL'S JUDGESHIP**

Shiloh

EPHRAIM

Bethel

Gilgal

Mizpah

Ramah

BENJAMIN

Gibeon

Gibeah

Jebus

R. Jordan

Dead Sea

Samuel's childhood in the Tabernacle
Samuel's residence as Judge
City where Samuel sat in judgment
Philistine attacks

# THE KINGDOM OF SAUL
## (I Samuel 8-31) 1025-1010 BCE

Saul began his reign over the Israelites in about 1025 BCE. At that time, the strongest and most important neighbouring nations of Egypt and Mesopotamia had split into many small independent kingdoms.

One of these were the Ammonites, who besieged the city of Jabesh-gilead, on the east side of the Jordan, soon after Saul had become king. Saul gathered around him a huge army and defeated the Ammonites and through this victory became popular amongst the people who saw him as a man of courage and strength. After this event Saul was anointed the first King of Israel by Samuel at Gilgal, which was near Saul's home town of Gibeah, and Samuel gave over his authority to Saul. After a time the Philistines again troubled the Israelites living in the area of Benjamin and became a threat to Saul whose eldest son, Jonathan, commanded some of the king's soldiers and wiped out the Philistine fortress at Geba. The rest of Saul's troops were stationed with him at Michmash and were soon to join his son at Geba; eventually Jonathan surprised the Philistines who began to panic and to flee in all directions.

Jonathan was hailed as a conqueror and hero, but for Saul there were still many battles to follow. Surrounded on all sides by enemies, he followed his success at Michmash with a series of victories over the Moabites, Ammonites, Edomites and others in the north. In the Negev, the south of the Holy Land, lived the Amalekites who constantly attacked the Israelites. Samuel the prophet ordered Saul to destroy them completely and not to spare even their king or possessions as this had been the command of God.

The Amalekites had tormented the Israelites even before they entered the Holy Land. Saul did not find it difficult to carry out Samuel's orders but he spared Agag, king of the Amalekites, together with some sheep and cattle. When Samuel heard of this he protested to Saul for not carrying out God's command. After this incident Samuel and Saul were never to see each other again.

Before leaving, Samuel told Saul that because of his disobedience of God's command he would be replaced as king of the Israelites by someone else, but Samuel did not mention

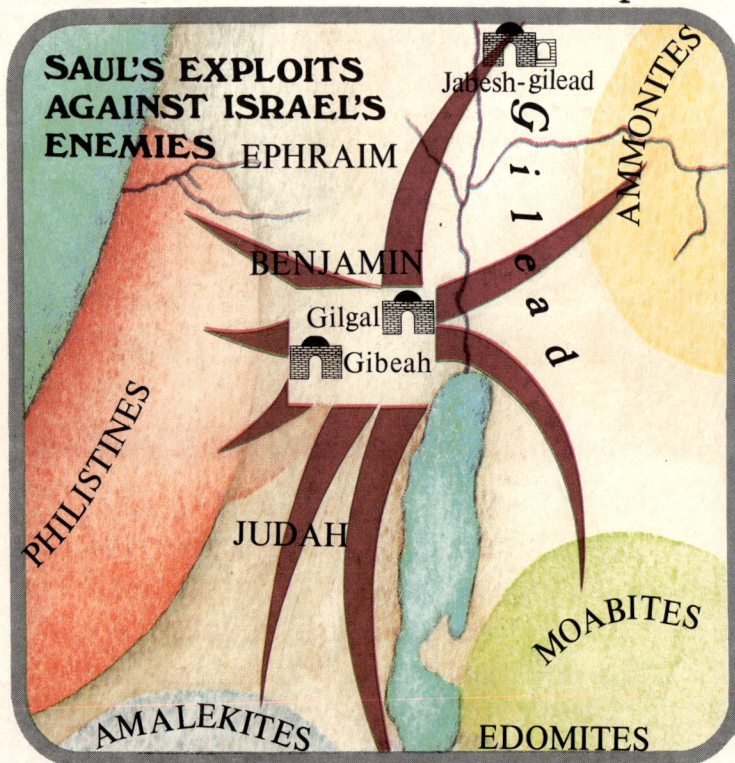

SAUL'S EXPLOITS AGAINST ISRAEL'S ENEMIES

Jabesh-gilead
EPHRAIM
AMMONITES
Gilead
BENJAMIN
Gilgal
Gibeah
PHILISTINES
JUDAH
MOABITES
AMALEKITES
EDOMITES

THE BATTLE OF MICHMASH

PHILISTINES
Mizpah
Michmash
Geba
Gilgal
SAUL
BENJAMIN
Gibeah
JONATHAN
Jebus

the future king by name. It so happened that this person was the young man from Bethlehem who had become a hero amongst the people, having killed Goliath, the giant and champion of the Philistines in the vale of Elah. He was David, the son of Jesse. King Saul was so impressed by David's courage that the king gave his daughter as a wife to David whom Samuel had previously anointed secretly in the family circle in Bethlehem in Judah. David was also a gifted musician and poet who many times sang and played the harp before King Saul whenever the King was sad and depressed. In the meantime Saul, who began to wonder who would follow him as King over Israel, came to suspect David and became very jealous of him. Jonathan, Saul's son, who had become a very close friend, warned David of the King's anger and did everything possible to save David, who was constantly running away from the threats of Saul. David went to Ramah, where he stayed with Samuel, then to Gibeah; to the city of Nob near Jerusalem; to Gath in the land of the Philistines and then to Ziklag; to Adullam where the caves gave protection for a time; to Keilah then to Ziph and Maon and from there to En-gedi.

At En-gedi, Saul happened to rest and fall asleep in the very cave where David was hiding. Although David could have killed the King he would not harm God's anointed, so he cut off a piece of the King's royal robe and when Saul awoke David showed him the material which proved that he had spared the King's life. Saul was impressed by this act of mercy and kindness and promised

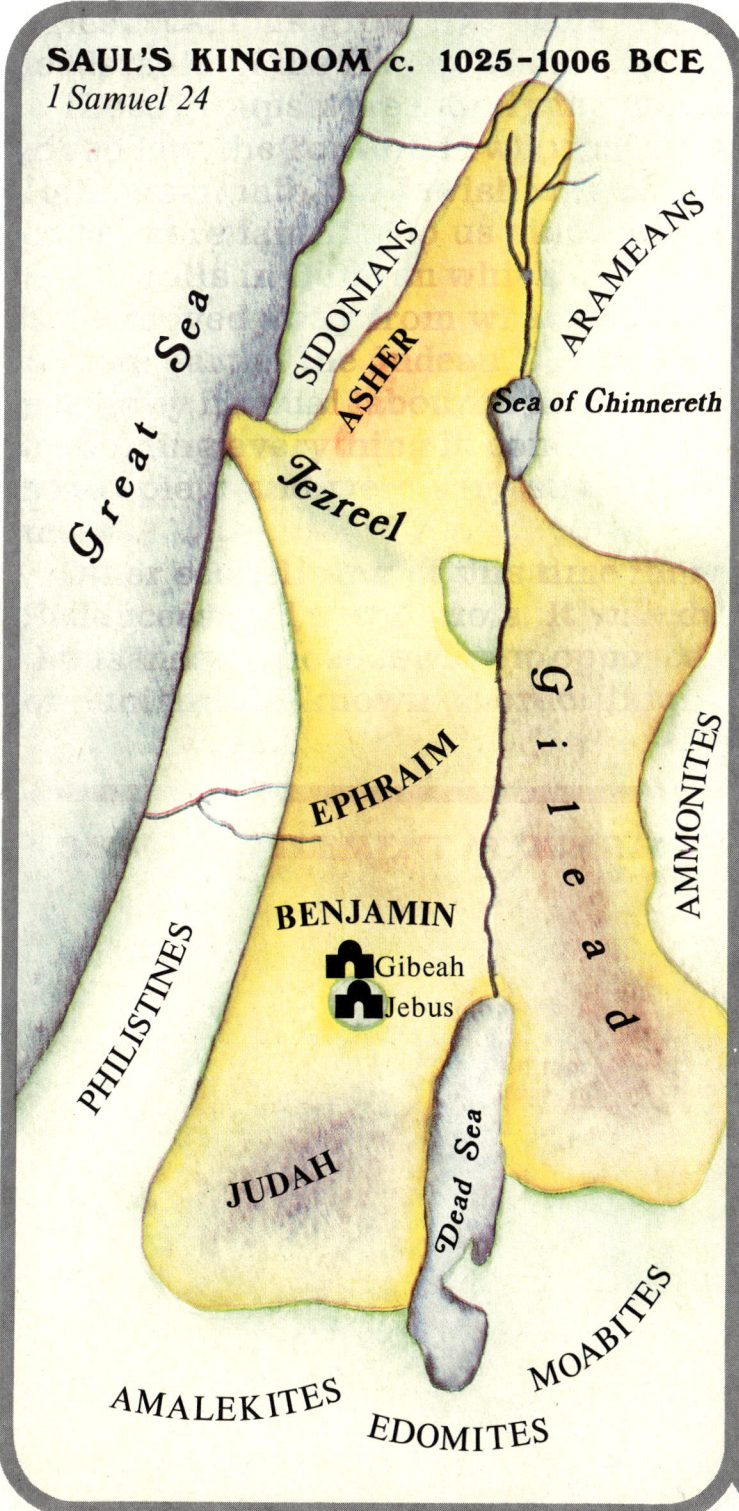

SAUL'S KINGDOM c. 1025-1006 BCE
1 Samuel 24

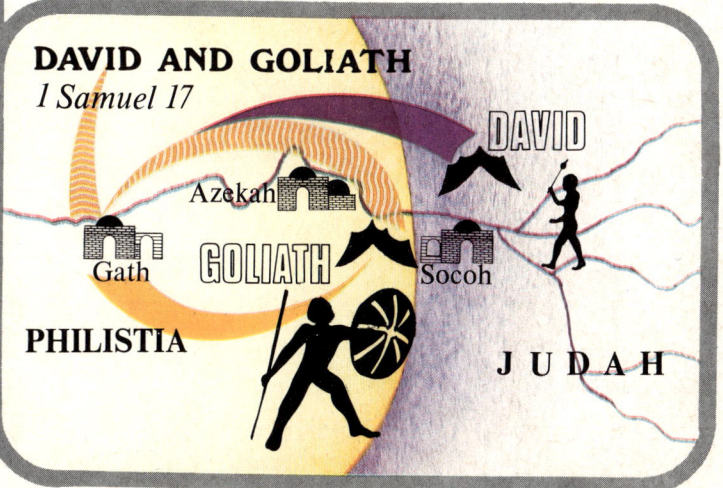

DAVID AND GOLIATH
1 Samuel 17

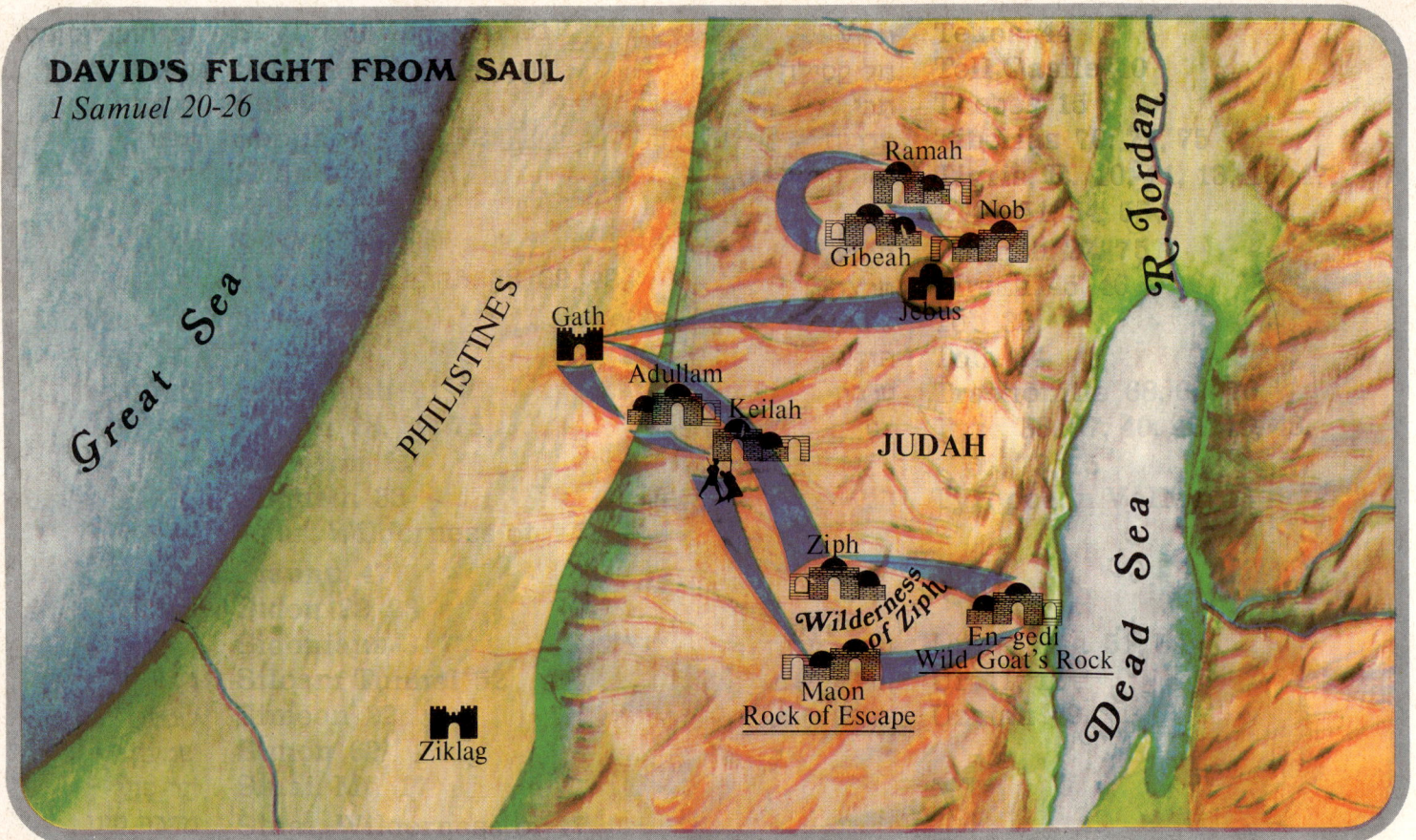

not to pursue David any longer, but David remained in En-gedi for a considerable time. Meanwhile Samuel the prophet died and was mourned by all Israel. He was buried in the fields of his home in Ramah.

Again becoming very jealous when told that David had been anointed future king of Israel, Saul continued to hunt David. However, David had many friends who formed themselves into a small troop of soldiers and were constantly on the lookout for Saul and his men. David could not understand the reason for Saul's hatred against him, especially as he had shown only honour and respect for the King. On another occasion, David found the place where Saul and his commander-in-chief Abner, were asleep concealed at the back of a cave. David's men said that now was the chance to kill the King, but David was against this.

He crept forward, took away the King's spear and a cruse of water and quietly left the cave. He then climbed a hill across the valley and shouted out the name of Abner, waking both Abner and the King, who recognised David's voice and realised that the spear and cruse of water had been taken to show that David had been so close to the King yet had not harmed him. Saul admitted how wrong he had been in his feelings towards David and called out to him that he would pursue him no longer and that he would do David no harm in the future.

In the meantime the Philistines renewed their war against the Israelites. Saul gathered his army together at the mountains of Gilboa but did not feel at ease about the forthcoming battle and wanted to ask someone for advice. Samuel was no longer alive, so, in desperation, he disguised himself and consulted a witch who lived in En-dor and was said to be able to speak to the dead. Saul heard a voice through the lips of the woman, which he assumed was that of Samuel, which told him that God had given the kingdom to David and that the next day Saul and his sons would die.

Saul was shocked but was determined to fight bravely, as befits a brave king and leader of his people. As had been foretold, the next day the Philistines launched a fierce battle during which Saul was wounded. He asked his armour-bearer to stab him with his sword, but the armour-bearer refused to kill the king, so Saul fell on his own sword and died. His three sons, including David's friend Jonathan, also died in the battle and when the Philistines found the bodies of Saul and his sons they were hung on the walls of the city of Beth-shean. When the men of Jabesh-gilead heard of this, they crossed the Jordan by night, removed the bodies from the wall and carried them back home for a proper burial. When David heard the sad news he could not control his grief. He rent his clothes and wept over the death of Saul and Jonathan. David paid tribute to the first King of Israel and to his friend Jonathan. Saul had reigned over the Israelites for 15 years during which time he had faced the massive task of defending Israel's borders, hardly ever having any peace or royal satisfaction.

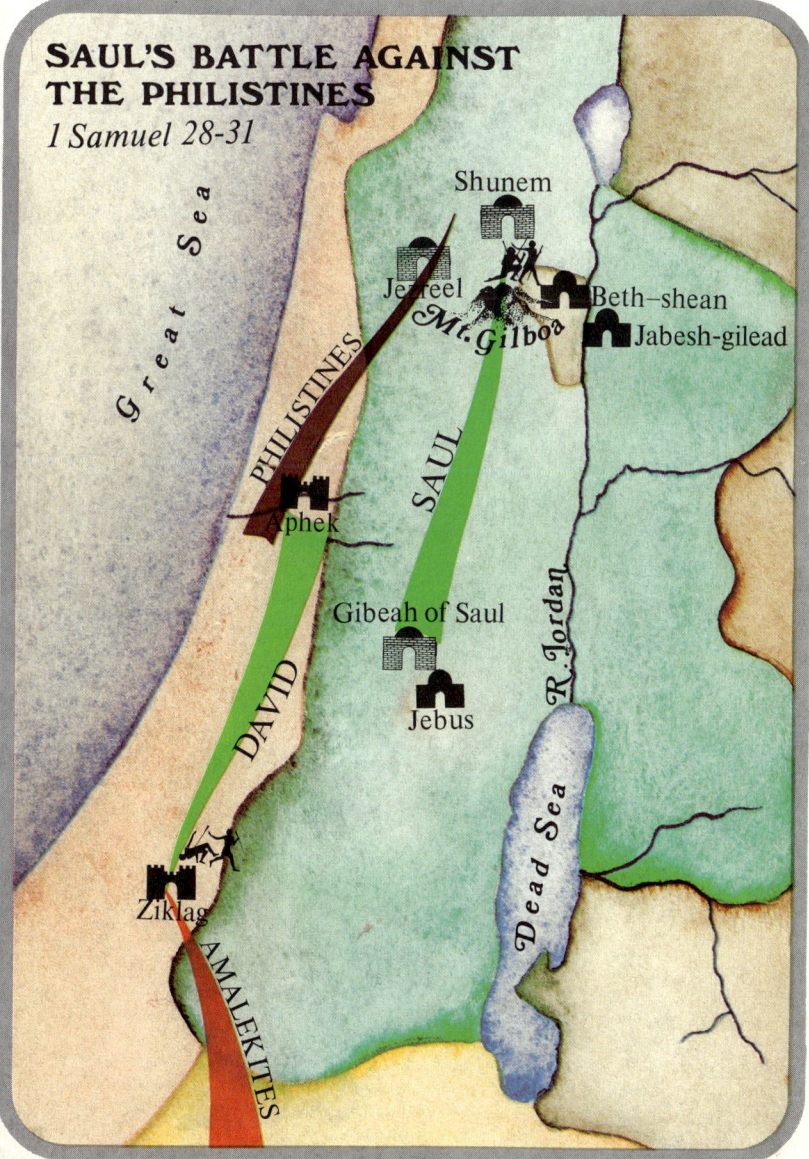

**SAUL'S BATTLE AGAINST THE PHILISTINES**
*1 Samuel 28-31*

## MONARCHY

**1030-1000 BCE**
Saul.

**1000-961 BCE**
David. Extension of Israelite sphere of influence up to River Euphrates.

**961-922 BCE**
Solomon.
Building of First Temple.

**922 BCE**
Split into Northern Kingdom of Israel and Southern Kingdom of Judah.
Strife between the two kingdoms.
Increasing pressure from Syria upon Northern Kingdom.

**722 BCE**
Fall of Northern Kingdom under Assyrian invasion.
Exile of ten tribes.

**586 BCE**
Fall of Jerusalem under Babylonian attack by Nebuchadnezzar.

**539 BCE**
Conquest of Babylon by Cyrus the Great — Persian Empire.

# THE KINGDOM OF DAVID

*(II Samuel 1-24; I Kings 1-2)*

1010-970 BCE

### THE KINGDOMS OF DAVID AND ESHBAAL
*2 Samuel 1-5*

ARAMEANS

ASHER

ZEBULUN

Great Sea

Beth-shean

ISRAEL
ESHBAAL

Gilead

Mahanaim

EPHRAIM

PHILISTINES

Gibeon

BENJAMIN

Jebus

Hebron

AMMON

JUDAH
DAVID

Ziklag

MOAB

### DAVID CONQUERS THE PHILISTINES
*2 Samuel 5:17-25*

Lower Beth-horon

ISRAEL

Upper Beth-horon

Gibeon

Gezer

Aijalon

Gibeah (Geba)

Jerusalem

Manahath

*Valley of Rephaim*

Baal-perazim

PHILISTINES

Beth-shemesh

Gath

Azekah

Bethlehem

JUDAH

Philistine attacks
Israelite force under David

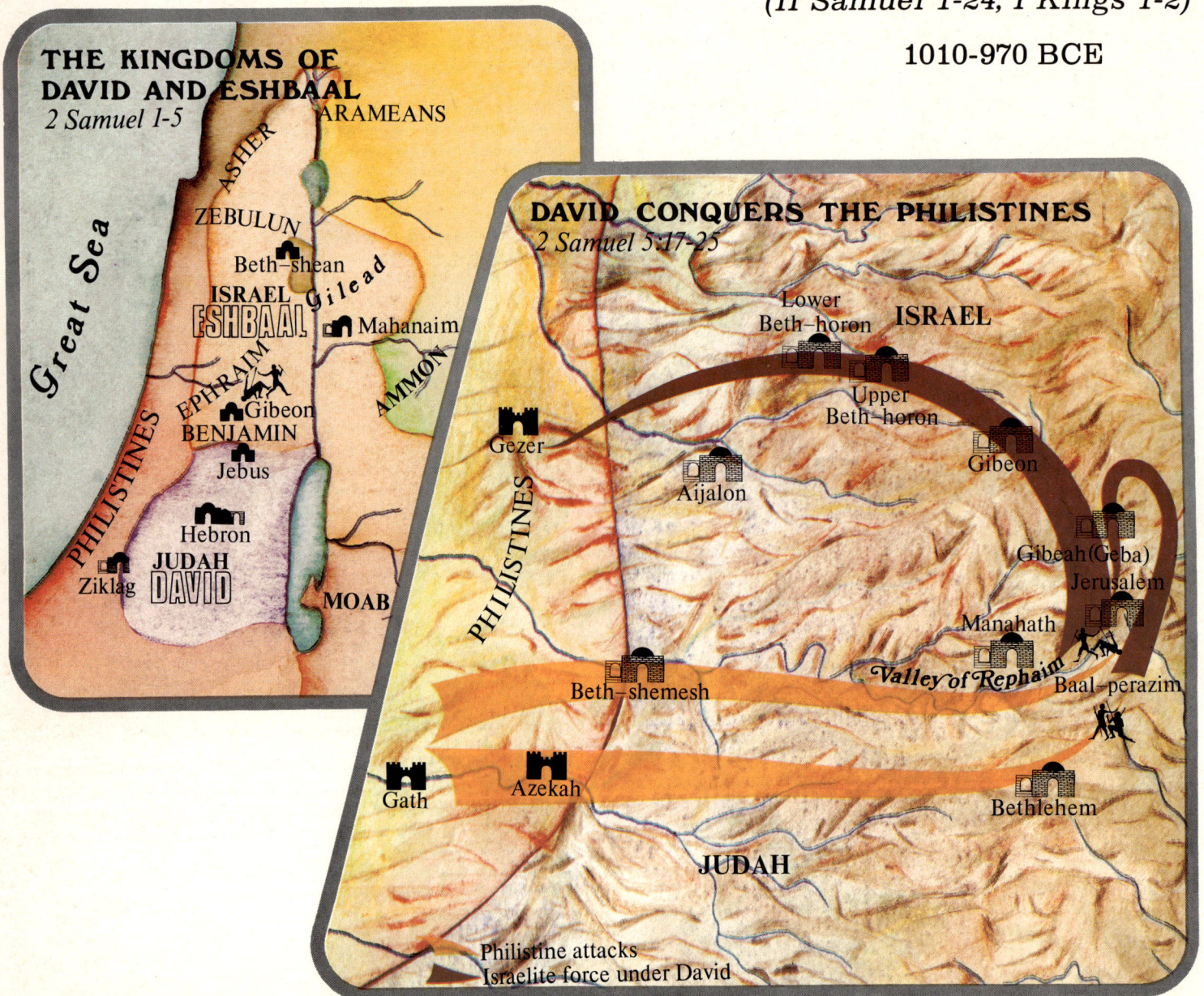

**K**ing Saul had one son who survived the battle of Gilboa whose name was Eshbaal, also known as Ish-Boshet. On Saul's death he was proclaimed the new king by Abner at Mahanaim. Some of the tribes remained loyal to Ish-Boshet but eventually he was killed by his own officers. The Elders from all the tribes came to David at Hebron asking him to become king of all Israel.

The neighbouring Philistines had heard about David's greatness as a leader and warrior and were not at all pleased on hearing the news that now he had been made king. In the meantime David decided to move his base from Hebron to Jerusalem which was at that time occupied by the Jebusites, who had made it into a strongly fortified city. Jerusalem stood on a hill and had many advantages needed for an important city as well as being centrally situated. Joab, the king's courageous commander, surprised the soldiers in the fortress and they surrendered. David entered the city and made it the capital of Israel naming the peak of the hill Mount Zion, and soon Jerusalem became known as 'the city of David'.

It was then that the Philistines decided to go to battle against David in order to try and prevent him from becoming too powerful. The Philistines occupied the Valley of Rephaim and made two attacks against the Israelites. In the second attempt David attacked them from the rear and drove the Philistines all the way to Gezer. The Philistines suffered enormous losses and soon they were to become David's subjects. By this time Jerusalem was established as Israel's capital city but David was not yet satisfied as he wanted it to be also the nation's religious centre. He went to Kiriath-jearim together with representatives of all the tribes to collect the Ark from the house of Abinadab where it had rested since the battle with the Philistines. Eventually the Ark was brought into Jerusalem on the shoulders of the Levites accompanied by music and singing. David wanted to build a permanent dwelling-place for the Ark, but the prophet Nathan said that David's son would construct such a building when there would be peace in the area. Nathan said that only a person who had not fought in wars and shed blood could build a Temple to house the Holy Ark.

David, who had agreed with what Nathan had said, built a fine pavilion for the Ark and ordered the Levites to sing praises to God whilst he himself composed the beautiful Psalms and became known as "The Sweet Singer of Israel". Jerusalem was now not only the capital city of the Israelites; the presence of the Ark of the Covenant made it also the Holy City and the central place for the worship of God. Under David's rule, a permanent army came into being, with every tribe sending a number of soldiers into the army which was commanded by Joab. David was successful in uniting the people and formulating laws which brought justice and righteousness to all the sections of the people of

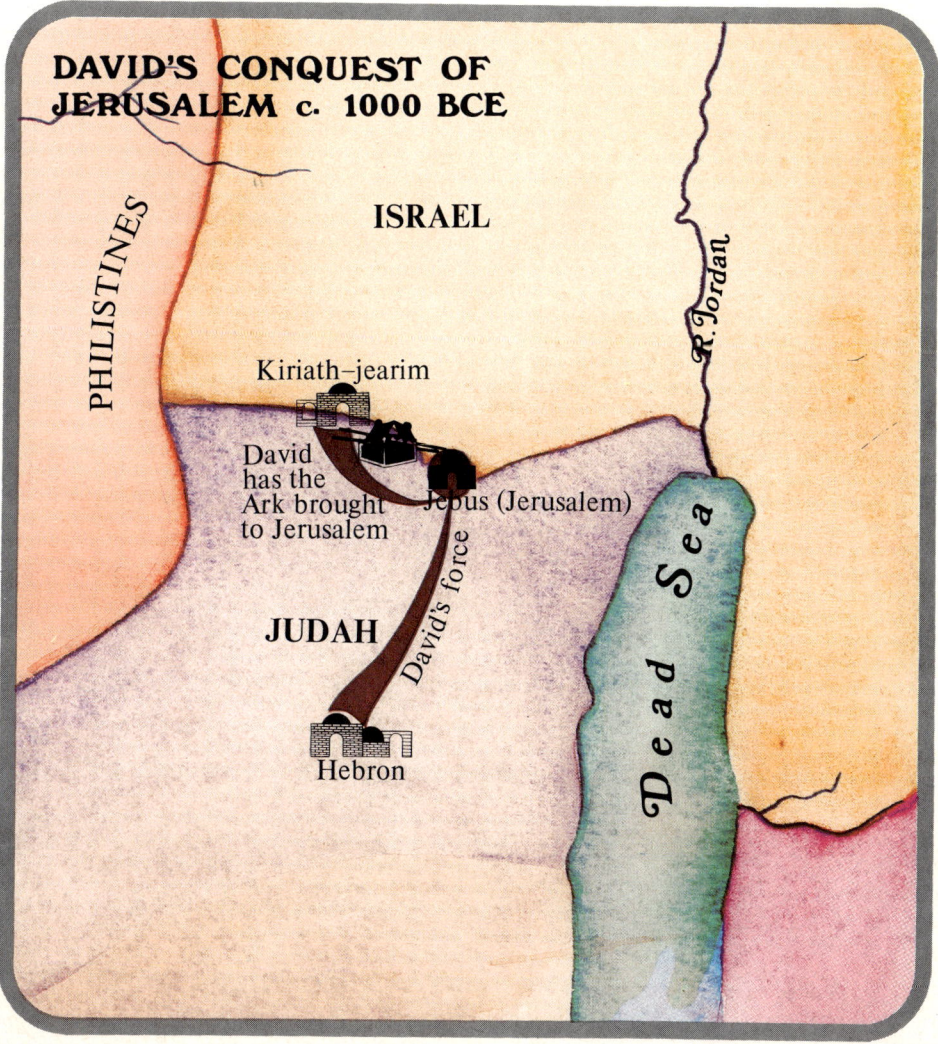

DAVID'S CONQUEST OF JERUSALEM c. 1000 BCE

PHILISTINES

ISRAEL

R. Jordan

Kiriath-jearim

David has the Ark brought to Jerusalem

Jebus (Jerusalem)

David's force

JUDAH

Dead Sea

Hebron

**DAVID EXPANDS HIS KINGDOM**
*2 Samuel 8:1-8*

Israel. A council of advisers and judges were appointed, and the principal priests were Zadok and Abiathar who were direct descendants of the first High Priest, Aaron. David also formed a special choir, consisting of Levites, who sang songs of praise and thanksgiving to God during the fixed services of worship.

Meanwhile David realised that he must destroy the power of the surrounding nations if the country's frontiers were to be protected against possible invaders. He fought against the Philistines and captured Gath, then David attacked the Amalekites, Edomites, Moabites and Ammonites who fled to Rabbah, their capital, going as far north as Damascus in Aram-zobah. So it was that David became master of the land from Elath in the south to Hamath in the north, the whole of Transjordan making a trade alliance with the Phoenicians who lived by the sea. Hyram, the king of Tyre, imported grain from David's kingdom and David in turn hired Phoenician architects, carpenters and masons to build Jerusalem into a beautiful capital city of Israel. Hiram also sent cedar-wood from Lebanon to Jerusalem for the building of David's palace, and the two kings became very friendly and assisted each other in many ways.

David's fame as a warrior spread his name far and wide, but during the campaign against the Ammonites, King David fell in love with a very beautiful woman whose name was Bathsheba, the wife of Uriah, a soldier under the command of David's general, Joab. David ordered Joab to place Uriah in the front lines of the battle and soon Uriah was killed. David was now free to marry Bathsheba, but it was not long before Nathan the prophet appeared at the palace and accused David of an outrageous crime and sin against God's laws which would result in serious consequences in the future. The king was filled with sorrow and anguish.

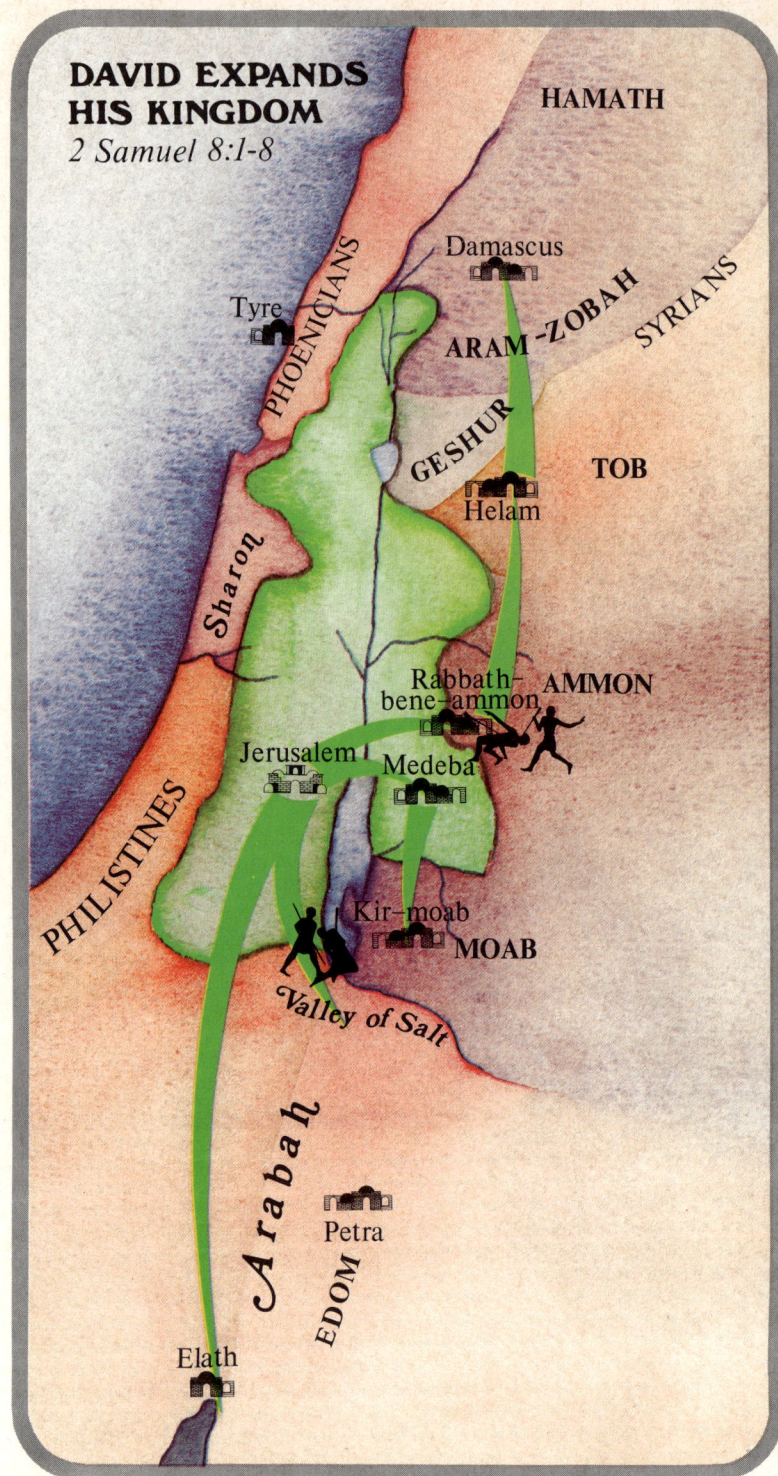

From this time onward, David's reign was very much clouded by tragedy within his own family circle. David had no peace or rest and great unhappiness was brought on him by his children. First his son Absalom killed his own brother, Amnon, during a bitter quarrel between the two brothers. Absalom was forced to escape from the anger of his father, King David, and for two years they did not see each other, but David could not restrain himself any longer and pardoned the handsome Absalom. However, the son showed no gratitude to his father the king and Absalom very soon began craftily plotting against the throne. Surrounding himself with a large number of supporters, Absalom conspired against the king and organised a rebellion. He asked David if he could go to Hebron to offer a sacrifice in David's former capital city. David agreed to the request, and when Absalom arrived there it was arranged that this would be the signal to rebel against the king in Jerusalem. David was caught by surprise and together with his men was forced to flee from Jerusalem. The two forces met at Mahanaim and a great battle commenced in which Absalom's soldiers suffered a tremendous defeat. Absalom, trying to escape on his mule, was caught in the thick branches of an oak tree by his long and flowing hair. The mule continued running but Absalom was left completely helpless hanging suspended in the air. The incident was reported to Joab who ordered soldiers to kill the rebel whilst hanging from the tree. David on hearing the news, broke down

### THE KINGDOM OF DAVID

HAMATH

ARAM-ZOBAH

ARAM-DAMASCUS

Damascus

SIDONIANS

Tyre

MAACAH

GESHUR

Great Sea

Megiddo

ISRAEL

AMMON

Gath

Jerusalem

PHILISTINES

JUDAH

Beer-sheba

MOAB

Desert

EDOM

Elath

········· Judah and Israel
::::::::: Territory conquered by David

and cried bitterly for the love that he had for Absalom despite his son's ingratitude towards him.

David returned to Jerusalem to continue ruling over Israel. Further rebellion was to follow. A Benjamite named Sheba rallied round his flag people who felt that David no longer had any authority over Israel. Again it was Joab who brought down the rebellion by pursuing Sheba and his men to Abel-beth-maacah in the far north.

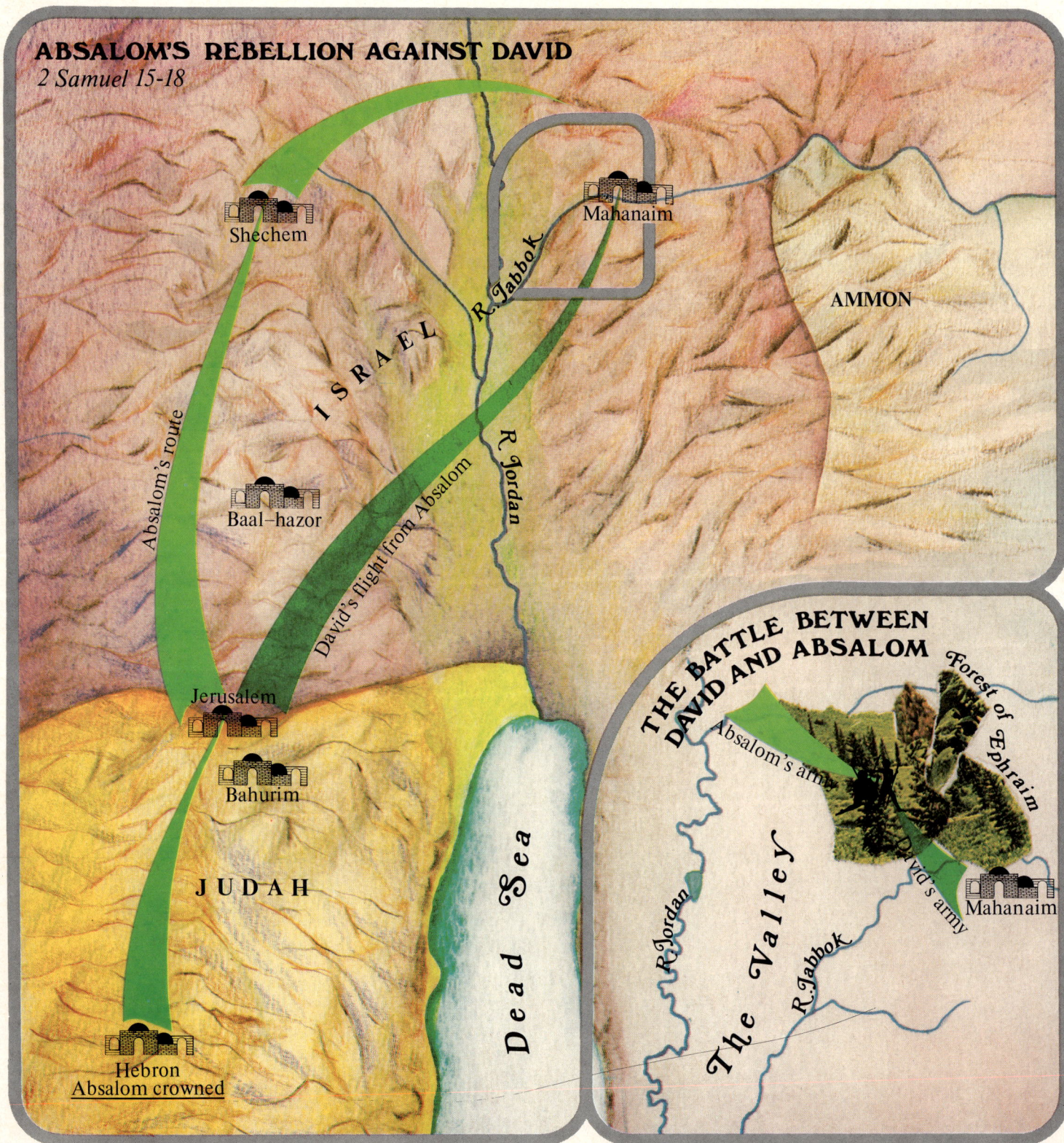

## ABSALOM'S REBELLION AGAINST DAVID
*2 Samuel 15-18*

Shechem

Mahanaim

AMMON

I S R A E L

R. Jabbok

Absalom's route

David's flight from Absalom

R. Jordan

Baal–hazor

Jerusalem

Bahurim

J U D A H

Dead Sea

Hebron
Absalom crowned

### THE BATTLE BETWEEN DAVID AND ABSALOM

Forest of Ephraim

Absalom's army

David's army

Mahanaim

The Valley

R. Jordan

R. Jabbok

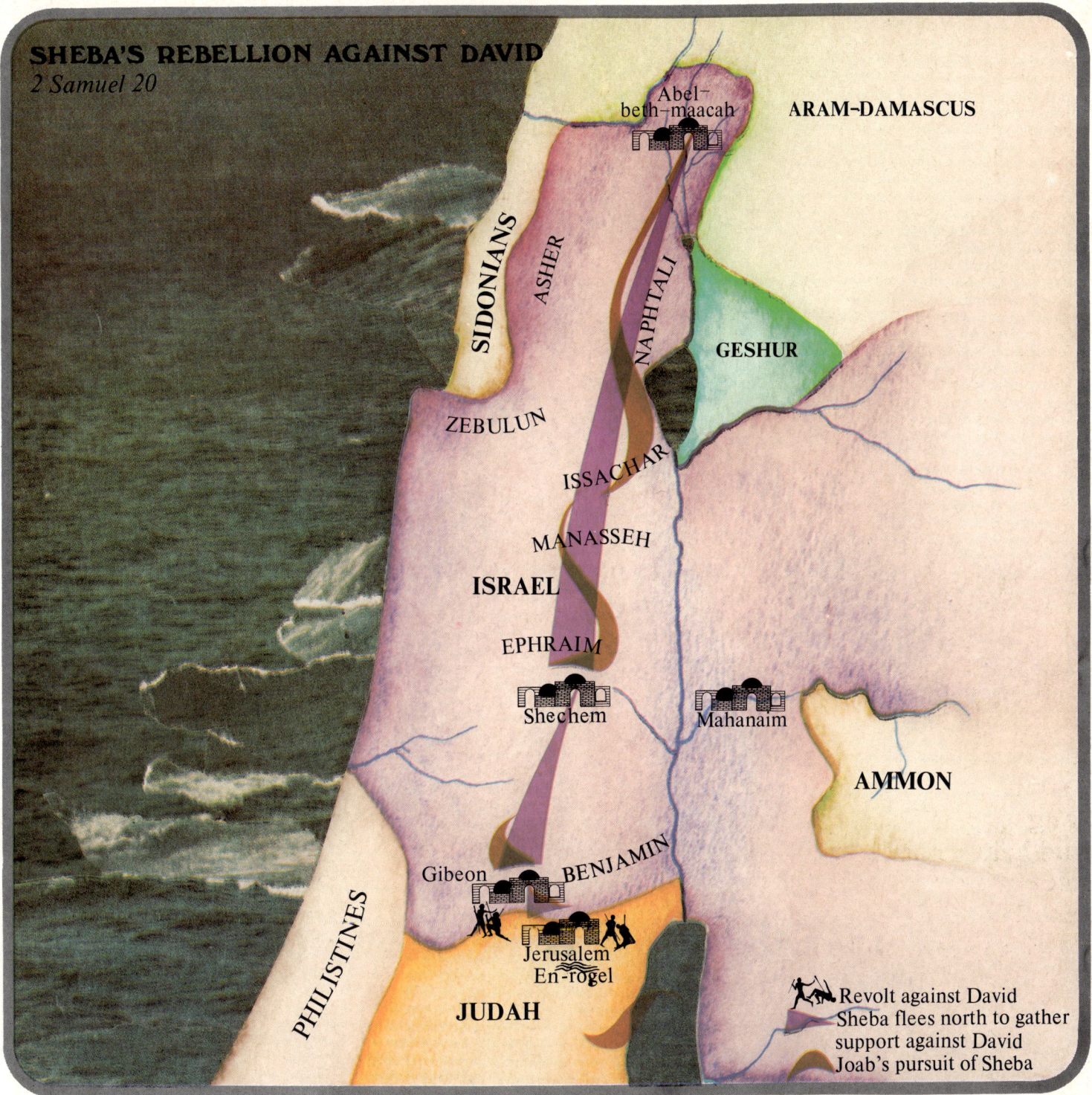

**SHEBA'S REBELLION AGAINST DAVID**
*2 Samuel 20*

ARAM-DAMASCUS

Abel-beth-maacah

SIDONIANS

ASHER

NAPHTALI

GESHUR

ZEBULUN

ISSACHAR

MANASSEH

ISRAEL

EPHRAIM

Shechem

Mahanaim

AMMON

Gibeon

BENJAMIN

Jerusalem
En-rogel

PHILISTINES

JUDAH

Revolt against David
Sheba flees north to gather
support against David
Joab's pursuit of Sheba

David had ruled his people for 40 years and it was time to hand over to his son Solomon. Zadok the high priest and Nathan the prophet were ordered by David to anoint the new king. When he was about to die, David told his son that he would be privileged to build God's Temple and called on Solomon to be strong and brave and remember to walk in God's ways and keep His commandments. Not long after this father-to-son talk, David died and was buried in his own beloved capital Jerusalem, the City of David.

# THE REIGN OF SOLOMON

## (I Kings 2-11)
### 970-930 BCE

In 970 BCE the young Solomon assumed the royal leadership of the Israelites. It was very soon after Solomon had become ruler that he went to the Tabernacle at Gibeon to lead a service of worship and offer sacrifices. During the night God appeared to him in a dream and asked Solomon if there was anything special that he wanted. Solomon did not request riches, glory or long life but only an understanding heart in order to rule in a just and wise manner. God promised to grant the king his wishes and also bless him with wealth, glory and a good life as Solomon had not asked selfishly for these gifts. The next morning the king returned to Jerusalem and offered prayers of thanksgiving to God followed by a great celebration.

Solomon very soon became known as the wisest of all men. He composed proverbs and songs and spoke the language of beasts and birds. Princes and kings came from near and far to hear his wise words and to listen to his beautiful fables and parables. His wisdom was put to the test constantly.

On one occasion, two women came before Solomon for his judgement on the question of the true mother of a child. Both women had given birth to a baby but one of them had died and both women claimed that the living child was theirs. The king ordered one of his guards to draw his sword and divide the living baby in two so that each woman could have half.

The true mother pleaded for the child's life asking that it should be given to the other woman rather than be killed, whilst the false mother

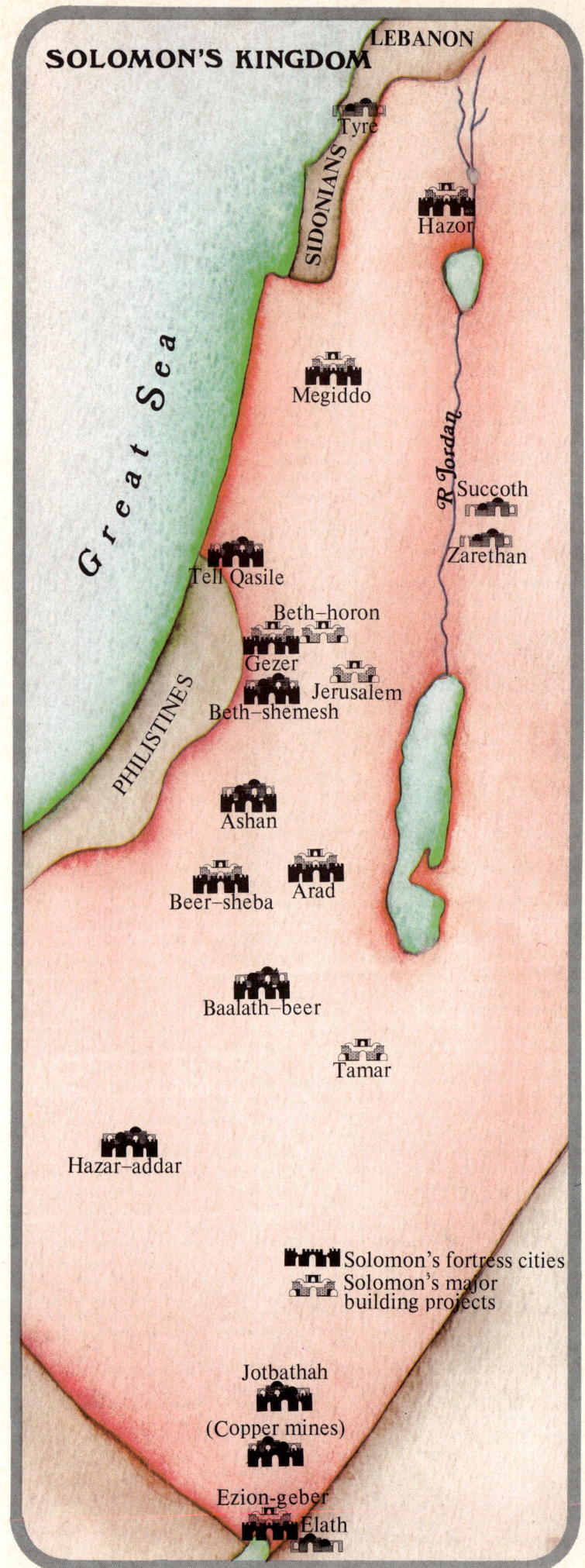

**SOLOMON'S KINGDOM**

LEBANON

SIDONIANS

Tyre

Hazor

Great Sea

Megiddo

R. Jordan

Succoth

Zarethan

Tell Qasile

Beth-horon

Gezer

Jerusalem

Beth-shemesh

PHILISTINES

Ashan

Beer-sheba    Arad

Baalath-beer

Tamar

Hazar-addar

Solomon's fortress cities
Solomon's major building projects

Jotbathah

(Copper mines)

Ezion-geber    Elath

agreed to the king's order. Solomon stopped the guard from killing the child and ordered the first woman to take the baby. It was obvious that she was the true mother.

During Solomon's reign the people of Israel lived in peace and prosperity. Merchants of neigbouring countries did business with the merchants of Israel who exported their own products and imported ivory, sandalwood, ebony, spices, gold, silver and pearls. Solomon possessed 40,000 stalls of horses for his 1,400 chariots which were all purchased from Egypt, some of which he sold to the Arameans and to the Hittites. But Solomon's greatest achievement came in the 14th year of his reign, 480 years after Israel's Exodus from Egypt, when he began to build the Temple which took seven and a half years to complete.

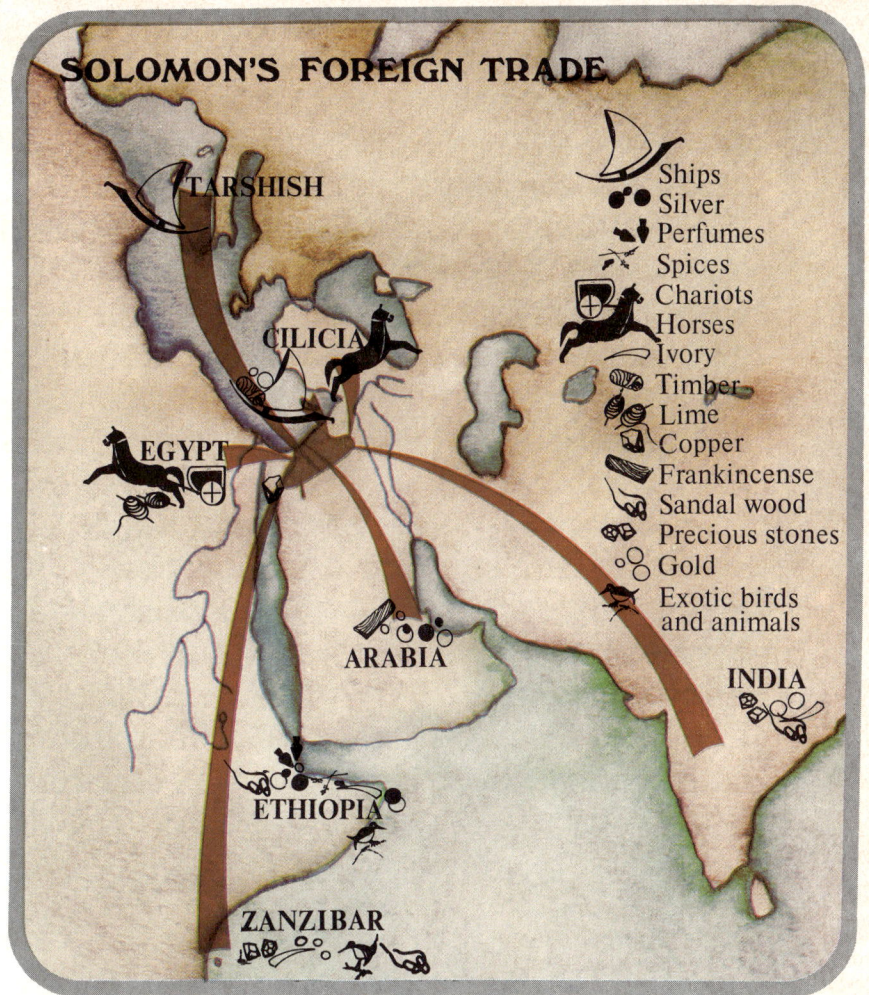

SOLOMON'S FOREIGN TRADE

Ships
Silver
Perfumes
Spices
Chariots
Horses
Ivory
Timber
Lime
Copper
Frankincense
Sandal wood
Precious stones
Gold
Exotic birds and animals

Hiram, king of Tyre, provided the skilled workmen, who designed and fashioned the brass work. Solomon sent in exchange vast quantities of barley, wheat, oil and wine to the Phoenicians. Thirty thousand Israelites were sent to Lebanon to cut down cedar and cypress trees from the mountain forests for the building of the Temple. When finished, the impressive and spacious Temple of God was a glorious sight on top of Mount Moriah, the Temple Mount. The preparation of stones and the brass was all done before they were brought to the Temple grounds so that the peace and serenity of Jerusalem would not be disturbed. The Temple like the Sanctuary in the Wilderness consisted of three parts.

The dedication of the Temple took place a week before the Festival of Tabernacles, on the eighth day of Tishri in the year 960 BCE. Hundreds of musicians and singers took part in the ceremony and celebrations which lasted for seven days followed by the Festival of Tabernacles. At the dedication ceremony the king and the people waited in the outer court while the Ark was brought into its permanent resting place in the Holy of Holies by the priests. Then the Temple was filled with a cloud, a visible sign of God's presence in the Temple. Solomon showed his gratitude for being allowed to fulfil God's promise to his father David that his son would build the Temple.

As the years went on Solomon succeeded in his commercial activities and also imposed heavy taxation on his people. The wealth allowed him to build magnificent palaces and buildings. His throne, which was elevated on six

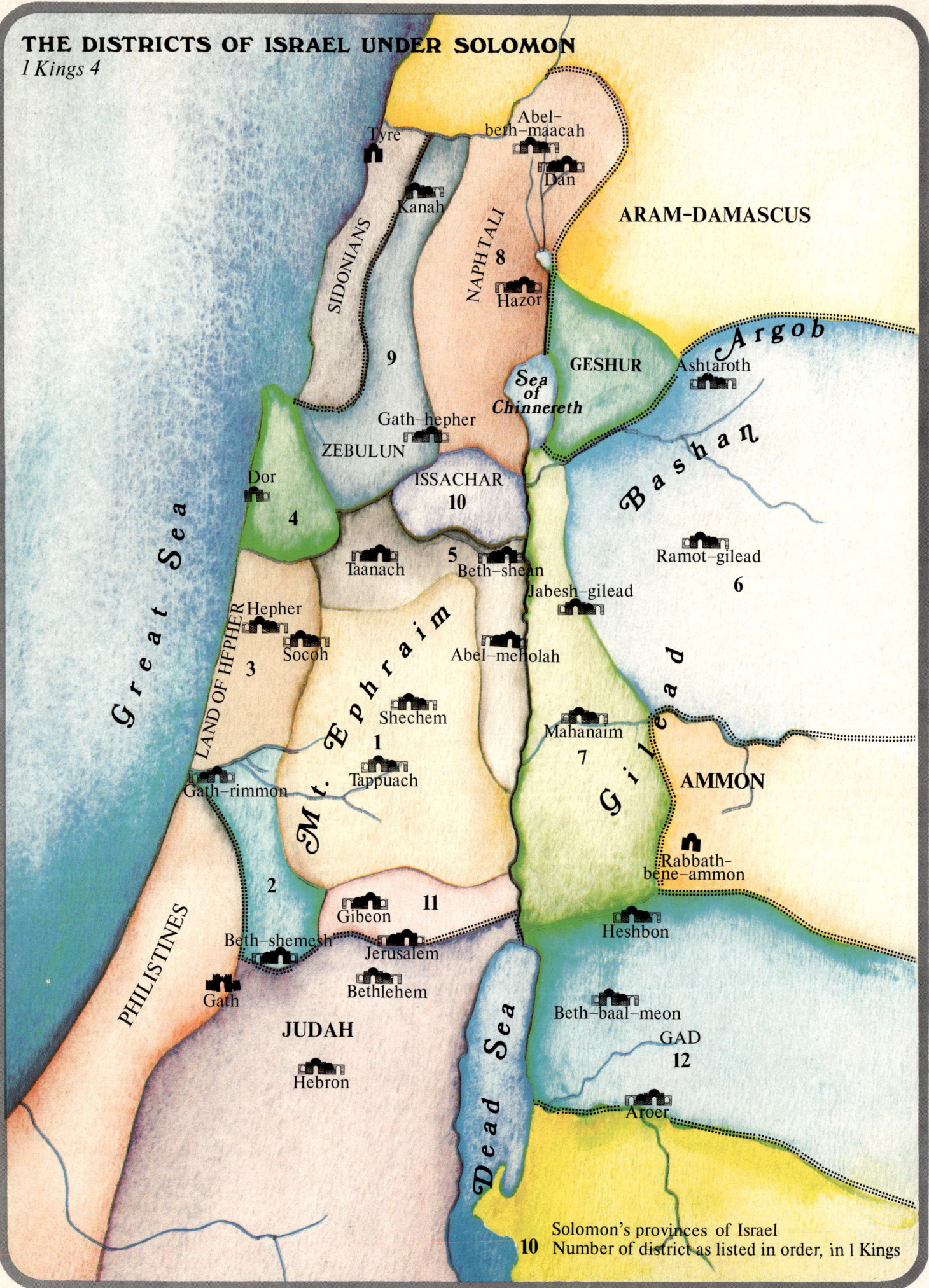

# THE DISTRICTS OF ISRAEL UNDER SOLOMON

*1 Kings 4*

Great Sea

Tyre

Abel-
beth-maacah

Dan

SIDONIANS

Kanah

ARAM-DAMASCUS

NAPHTALI

8

Hazor

9

Argob

GESHUR

Ashtaroth

Sea
of
Chinnereth

Gath-hepher

ZEBULUN

Bashan

Dor

ISSACHAR

10

4

Taanach

5

Beth-shean

Ramot-gilead

6

Jabesh-gilead

LAND OF HEPHER

Hepher

Socoh

Abel-meholah

3

Mt. Ephraim

Shechem

Mahanaim

Gilead

1

7

Gath-rimmon

Tappuach

AMMON

2

Gibeon

11

Rabbath-
bene-ammon

Beth-shemesh

Jerusalem

Heshbon

Gath

Bethlehem

Beth-baal-meon

PHILISTINES

JUDAH

GAD

12

Hebron

Dead Sea

Aroer

Solomon's provinces of Israel

**10** Number of district as listed in order, in 1 Kings

42

steps, was made of ivory covered with gold and all drinking vessels were of pure gold. Solomon's trade relations with other countries increased through the fleet of ships which he had ordered to be constructed and which were stationed at the port of Ezion-geber, near Elath. Recent excavations at this site reveal a copper refinery and mining industry which must have provided a sizeable income for Solomon.

The king's wisdom became known everywhere and important personalities and leaders came to visit him. Amongst these was the Queen of Sheba who wanted to see for herself all the wonderful things she had heard about Solomon, the Temple and the glorious buildings. All that the queen saw and heard impressed her greatly and she returned to her own land with much admiration for the king of Israel. However, as time went on there were many things in Solomon's deeds which upset the people of Israel. The heavy taxes and the hard work needed to maintain the king's standard of living, together with the many foreign wives he had married, angered and embittered the people throughout the country. The Lord was also displeased with Solomon's actions and through the prophet Ahijah the king was told that after his death the kingdom would be divided. The prophet met Jeroboam, one of Solomon's officers, and told him that he would inherit ten parts of the kingdom and two parts would be retained by Solomon's heir. When the king heard of this incident he wanted to kill Jeroboam but the officer fled and remained in Egypt until the king died.

Solomon's last years were troubled by revolts and outbreaks of war. The king who had shown such promise in the early years of his reign ended his life unhappy and disappointed. Neighbouring princes waited for a chance to rebel against Solomon as they had become jealous of the king's wisdom, wealth and success. The wise king Solomon died after ruling the people of Israel for 40 years and was laid to rest in the royal burial ground in Jerusalem where he had built the Temple which was to last for 400 years, the Western Wall — Kotel Ma'aravi — being the only section standing to this day.

SOLOMON'S JERUSALEM

Tyropoeon Valley

Solomon's city walls

Temple

Palace

Solomon's addition

The Jebusite and David's city

En-gihon

Pool of Siloam

| Division of Kingdom | 933 BCE |
| Ahab | 876-853 BCE |
| Elijah | 870 BCE |
| Amos & Hosea (prophetic activity) | 760-734 BCE |
| Isaiah | 740 BCE |
| Micah | 740 BCE |

# THE DIVISION OF THE KINGDOM
### (I Kings 12-16; II Chronicles 10-16)
#### 930-880 BCE

It was not long after Solomon's death that Ahijah's prophecy became true and the Holy Land was divided into two separate kingdoms, that of the northern part being the Kingdom of Israel which existed for almost 250 years, and the southern part of the Kingdom of Judah which lasted for over 340 years. All this could have been avoided had Rehoboam, Solomon's son and successor, listened to advice given to him to discontinue the heavy taxation and forced labour which his father had introduced. The people rebelled against this and the ten tribes of the new Kingdom of Israel made Jeroboam, from the tribe of Ephraim, their first king. Rehoboam remained king of Judah, and the crown was handed down from father to son. Many of the kings were noted for their righteousness and justice. However, in the Kingdom of Israel the kings did much which was evil in the eyes of God. Jeroboam introduced idol worship in Dan and Bethel in order to prevent his subjects from returning to the Holy City of Jerusalem, which was in the Kingdom of Judah, for worship. Jeroboam's bad example, which was followed by those kings who reigned after him, led to the eventual defeat and dispersion of the Kingdom of Israel in the year 721 BCE.

The Kingdom of Judah remained, as God had promised, with a permanent dynasty of David to the very end of the kingdom. Soon after Rehoboam had been made king an attack was made on his kingdom by Shishak, the king of Egypt, who also attacked the Kingdom of Israel, but then withdrew his army and took away with him treasures from the Temple in Jerusalem, which included the golden shields of Solomon. All this came about as the people practised idolatry and did not go in the ways of God. The prophet Shemaiah told the people to repent; they fol-

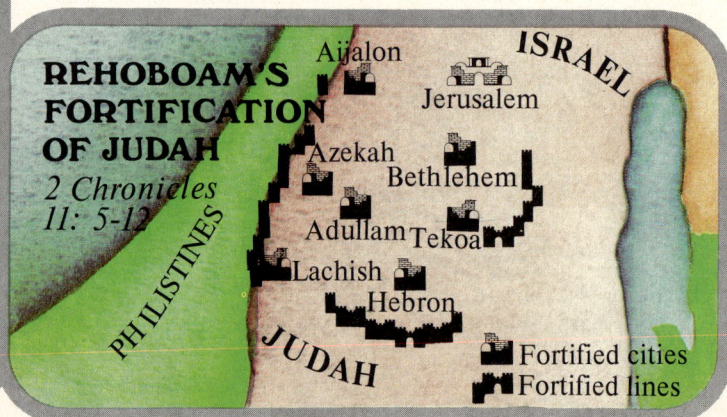

THE DIVISION OF THE KINGDOM

Damascus
Dan
ARAM-DAMASCUS
SIDONIANS
GESHUR
Kingdom of ISRAEL
Shechem
Bethel
Gath
Jerusalem
PHILISTINES
AMMON
Kingdom of JUDAH
MOAB
EDOM
Breakaway states

REHOBOAM'S FORTIFICATION OF JUDAH
2 Chronicles 11: 5-12
Aijalon
Jerusalem
ISRAEL
Azekah
Bethlehem
Adullam
Tekoa
Lachish
Hebron
PHILISTINES
JUDAH
■ Fortified cities
■ Fortified lines

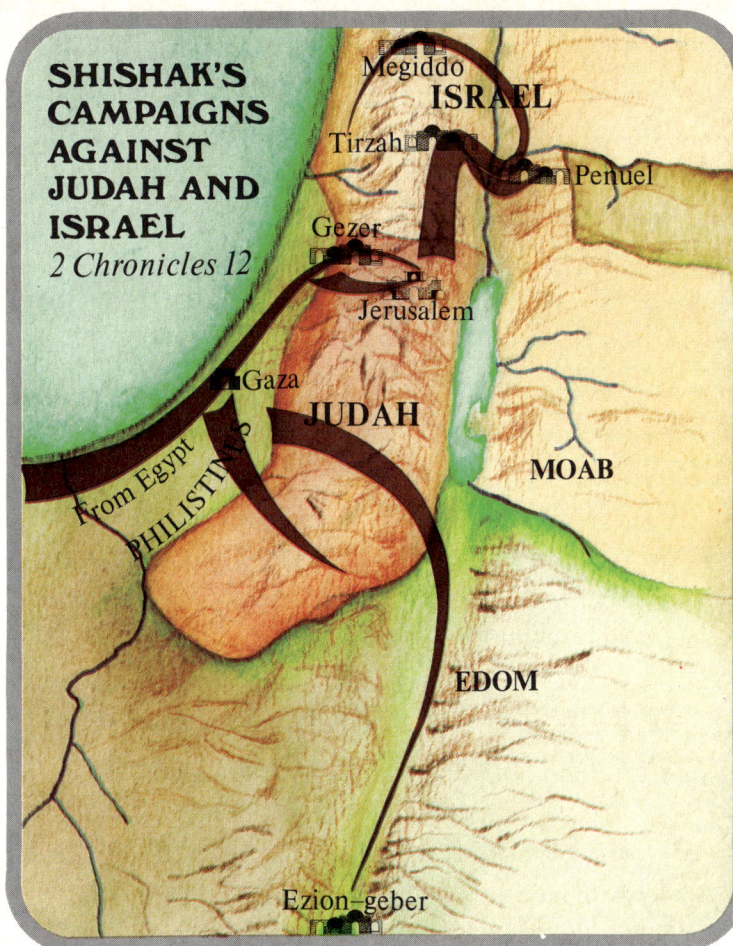

SHISHAK'S CAMPAIGNS AGAINST JUDAH AND ISRAEL
*2 Chronicles 12*

THE CONFLICT BETWEEN ASA AND BAASHA
*1 Kings 15:16-22*

Border area in dispute
Baasha's attack on Judah
Attack of Ben Hadad I on Israel

lowed his advice and peace returned to the land. However, the Kingdom of Judah was much weakened by the invasion of Shishak and decided to link up with the Aramean kingdom of Damascus, which would assist the Kingdom of Judah should the northern Kingdom of Israel decide to attack Judah.

It was not long before such a situation became a reality. Asa, the pious King of Judah, decided to destroy idolatry in his land. In the meantime, Baasha, king of the Kingdom of Israel, prepared to attack Judah and fortified the city of Ramah, in order to prevent his subjects going south to Jerusalem. When this happened Asa asked Ben Hadad I, the king of Damascus, to help him by invading the northern territory of Israel, which caused Baasha to withdraw his army from Ramah and stop his attacks on Judah, driving him back to his capital city, Tirzah. After this incident the boundary became the area between Geba and Mizpah.

But, by calling on Ben Hadad and not relying on the help of God, Asa made the greatest mistake of his life. For this lack of faith the prophet Hanani foretold constant wars for the rest of the king's life, and he died, having reigned for 41 years, in the City of David where he was buried. Jehoshaphat his son became king and followed the commandments of God. He soon sent priests, princes and Levites to all the cities of Judah to teach the people the Torah, the word of God, and the king received tribute and presents from the surrounding countries.

# THE RISE OF ASSYRIA AND FALL OF ISRAEL

*(I Kings 17-22; II King 1-17)*
880-721 BCE

It was around the year 885 BCE that Omri, a popular army general, became king of the northern kingdom of Israel and although he himself reigned for only 12 years he started a dynasty which lasted for 40 years. Omri was as sinful as his predecessors and when he came to power he transferred the capital from Tirzah to Samaria which stood high above the surrounding valley and proved to be a wise choice from the military point of view. Later he fought some wars against the Assyrians in which he lost a number of towns which had belonged to the northern kingdom. It is interesting to note that Omri was the first Hebrew king to be mentioned in inscriptions found in Assyria where the northern kingdom is described as being 'the land of the house of Omri'.

When Omri died his son Ahab became king. He married Jezebel who influenced the king to establish the idol-worship of Baal throughout Israel. At the same time in the southern kingdom of Judah, king Jehoshaphat banned any kind of idol-worship and was only concerned with the spread of the knowledge of God's laws. As a result of this he lived in peace with his neighbours and prospered in every way. Jehoshaphat formed an alliance with the kingdom of Israel and this was strengthened further by the marriage of his son Jehoram to the daughter of king Ahab.

In the meantime, the kingdom of Israel declined spiritually through Jezebel's encouragement of Baal-worship from her native land of Sidon. Ahab did nothing to stop the sinful behaviour of the

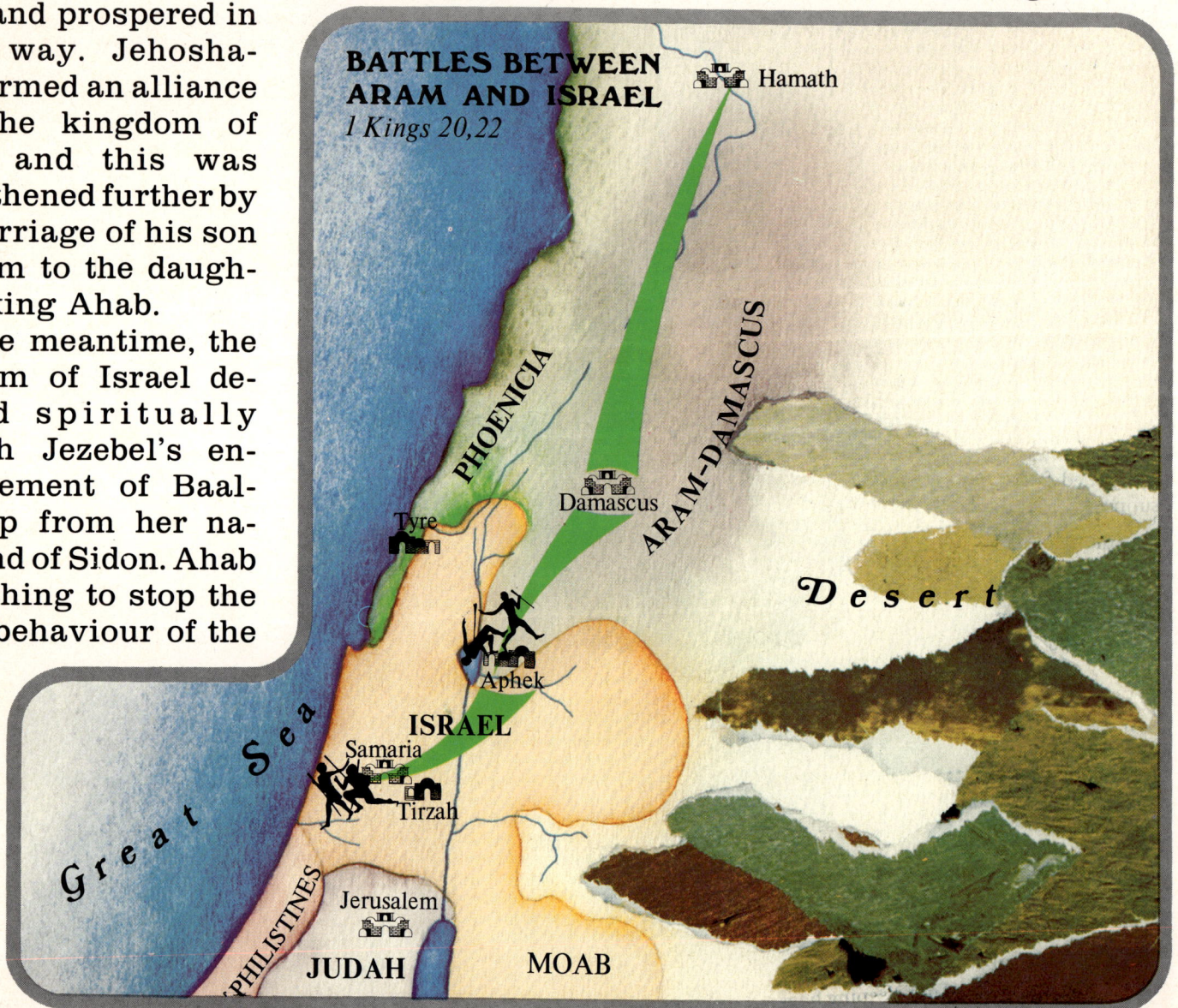

**BATTLES BETWEEN ARAM AND ISRAEL**
*1 Kings 20,22*

Hamath

PHOENICIA

ARAM-DAMASCUS

Damascus

Tyre

Desert

Aphek

ISRAEL

Samaria

Tirzah

Great Sea

Jerusalem

PHILISTINES

JUDAH

MOAB

people and it was not until the prophet Elijah from the town of Tishbe in Gilead confronted the king in God's name that Ahab was forced to arrange a trial between God and Baal on the peak of Mount Carmel. On one side stood all the prophets of Baal and on the other side Elijah stood alone, and the test which occurred proved to all present that the Lord was God and everything to do with Baal was false and must be destroyed. Eventually the prophet Elijah travelled to Mount Horeb where he had a vision and heard God tell him to continue his mission. Elijah felt that his work had all been worthwhile and that there was hope for the future of the Israelites. But soon the time came for Elijah to hand over his work to his successor Elisha. God had told Elijah to anoint Elisha of Abel-meholah as the next prophet of Israel and when Elijah had done this he was carried up into heaven by a whirlwind, vanishing into the sky.

Towards the end of king Ahab's life he was mainly occupied with great wars against Syria who had besieged Samaria the capital. Although Israel succeeded in regaining land which it had lost and enjoyed peace for a number of years, the campaigns against Israel by the Assyrians caused the fall of the northern kingdom of Israel. This situation had been foretold by the prophets Amos and Hosea who warned against an unjust society not in keeping with

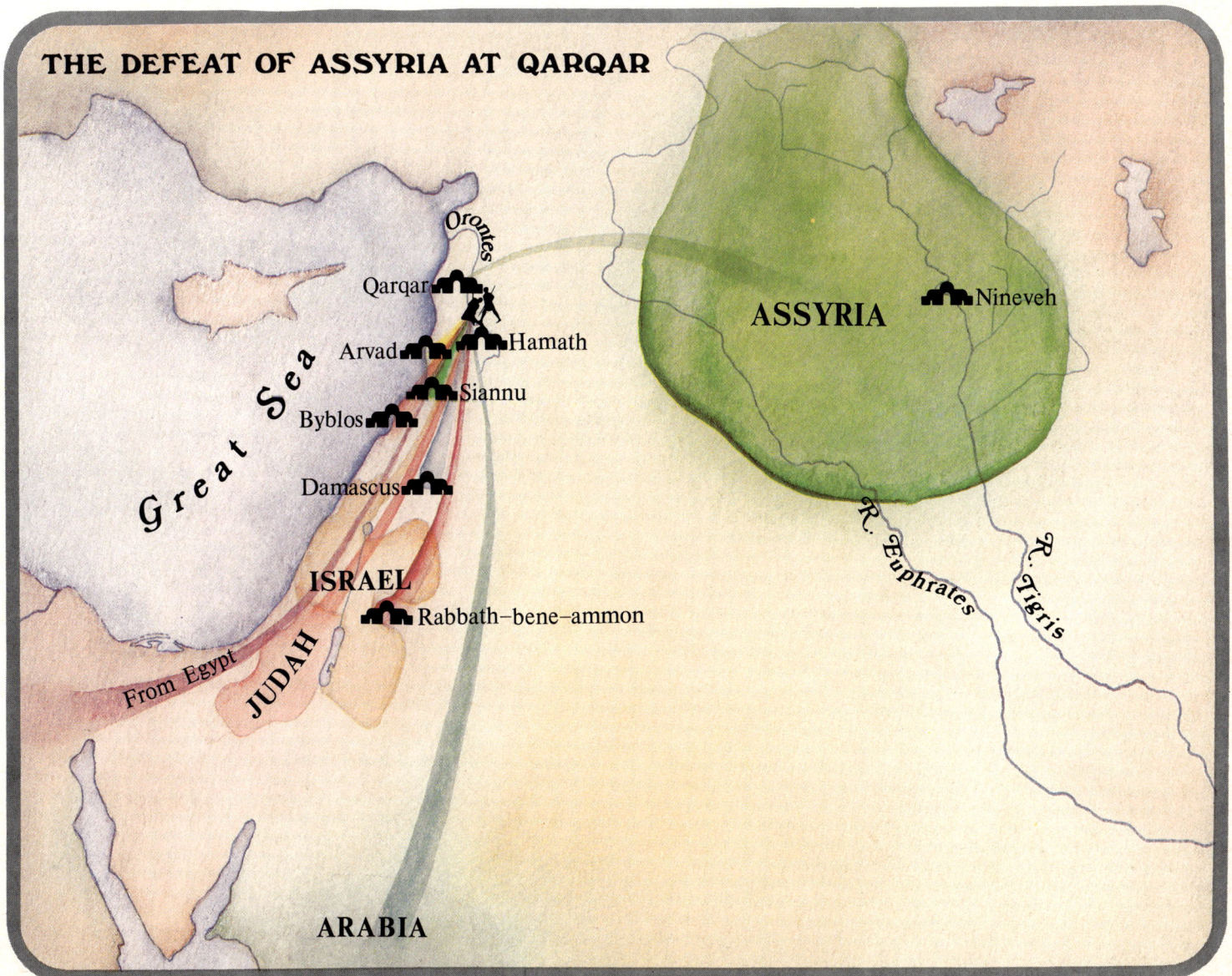

THE DEFEAT OF ASSYRIA AT QARQAR

Orontes
Qarqar
Arvad
Hamath
Siannu
Byblos
Damascus
ISRAEL
Rabbath–bene–ammon
Great Sea
From Egypt
JUDAH
ASSYRIA
Nineveh
R. Euphrates
R. Tigris
ARABIA

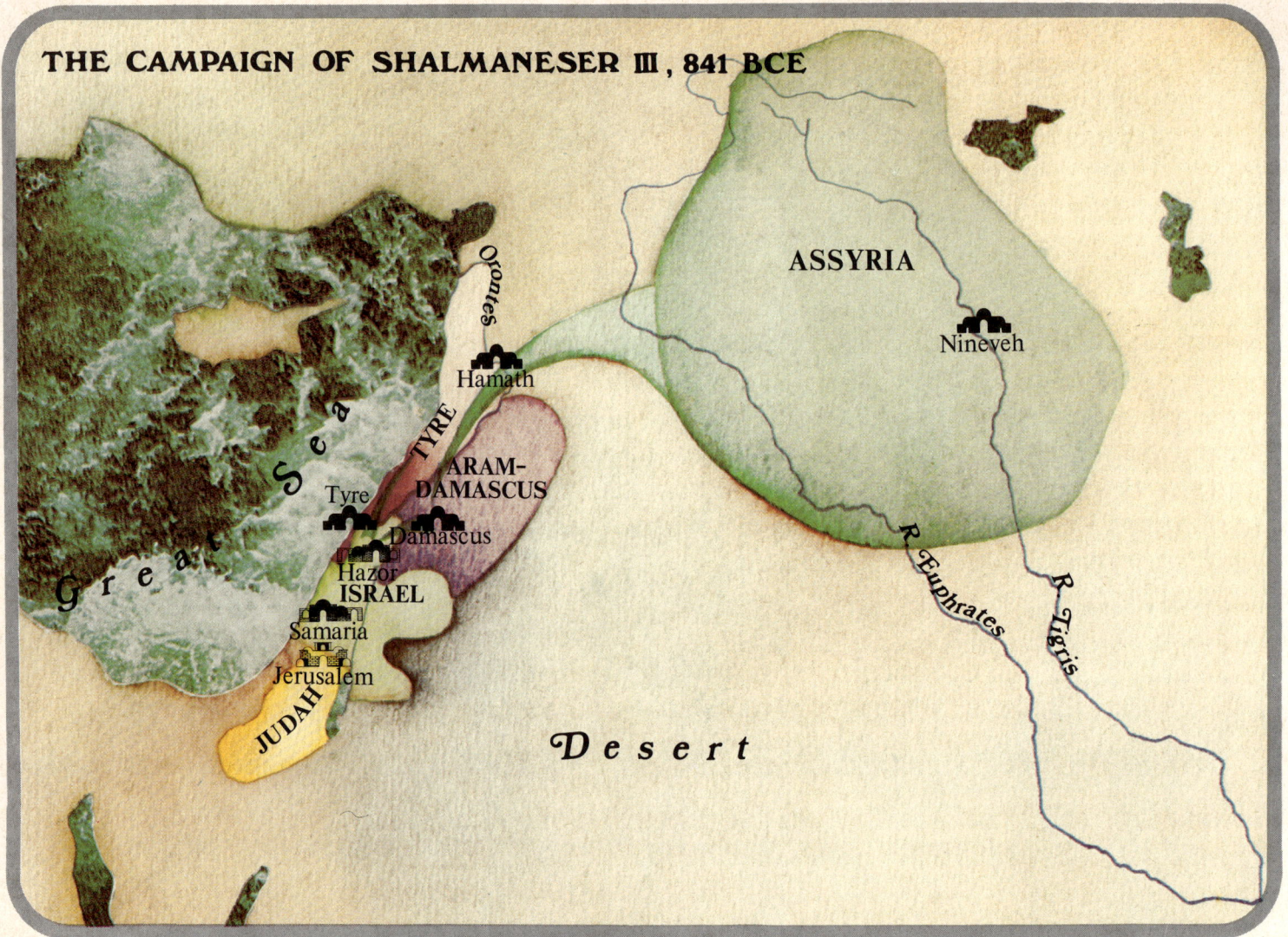

the commandments of God which would cause the collapse of the kingdom. Their words were not heard and disaster came to the kingdom of Israel with its captivity and downfall.

The Assyrian king Shalmaneser III was successful in leading his army from a point west of the River Tigris right across to the Mediterranean ('Great Sea') but was stopped just before getting to the coast at a place called Qarqar on the Syrian river of Orontes. The cause of defeat was the alliance of 12 kings which included king Ahab of Israel and Ben-Hadad the king of Damascus. Shalmaneser was forced to return home and no more was heard of him in that area for 12 years. By that time a new king, Jehu, was leader of Israel. He destroyed the whole house of Ahab and put an end to Baal-worship. In the meantime Israel's position in face of the Damascus rulers was becoming constantly weaker. All her areas east of the River Jordan were conquered and the Arameans had reached as far south as Gath on the Mediterranean coast although some of those areas were later regained when Damascus was raided by an Assyrian king, and Israel was allowed to live in peace and quiet for a short period.

In the southern kingdom of Judah the situation was not very much better. The ninth king Uzziah had made his kingdom wealthy and strong, but as in the northern kingdom prophets came with a strong message reminding the people that they had to live by a covenant which they had made with God. It was Micah and Isaiah who tried to arouse the inhabitants of Judah into a sense of responsibility.

King Uzziah reigned for 52 years. At the beginning of his reign he served God well and enjoyed prosperity for a considerable number of years. His military successes were many. Uzziah also did much to increase farming and agriculture, but towards the end of his reign his successes went to his head and caused his downfall. After an attack on the High Priest Azariah, the king was smitten with leprosy and was forced to live in isolation to the end of his days.

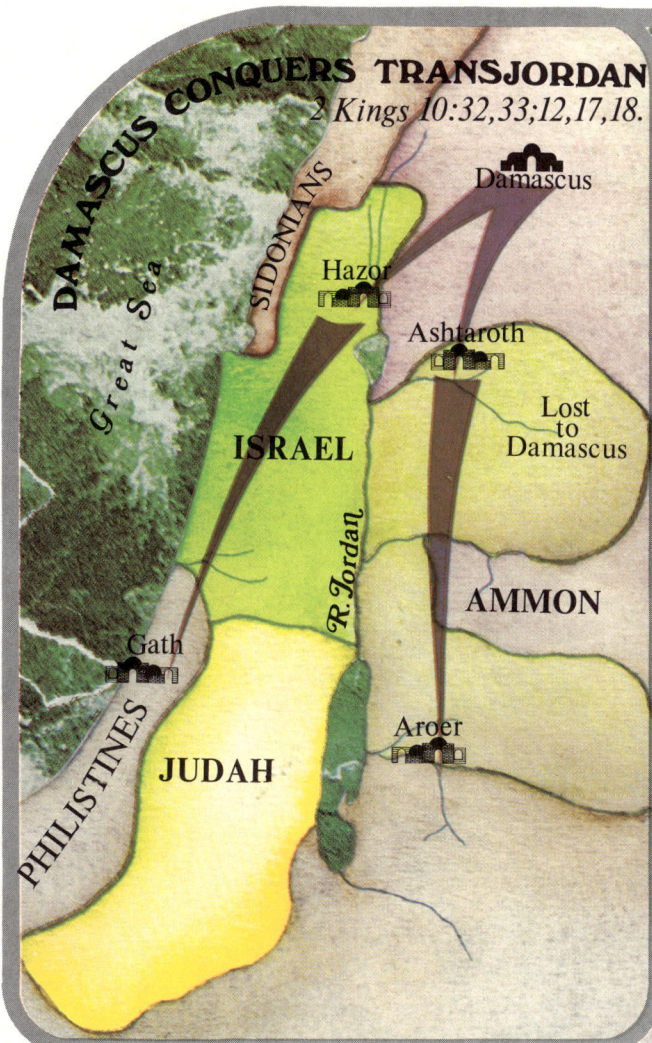

**DAMASCUS CONQUERS TRANSJORDAN**
*2 Kings 10:32,33;12,17,18.*

Great Sea

SIDONIANS

Damascus

Hazor

Ashtaroth

Lost to Damascus

**ISRAEL**

R. Jordan

**AMMON**

Gath

Aroer

PHILISTINES

**JUDAH**

**THE KINGDOMS OF JEROBOAM II AND UZZIAH**

SIDONIANS

Lebo–hamath

Great Sea

Damascus

**ISRAEL**
JEROBOAM

Samaria

Jerusalem

PHILISTINES

**JUDAH**
UZZIAH

Elath

The prophets Amos and Hosea preached their warnings to a society which had become morally and spiritually corrupt owing to the prosperity and luxury of the time. In their writings these two prophets describe the situation in the northern kingdom at that time.

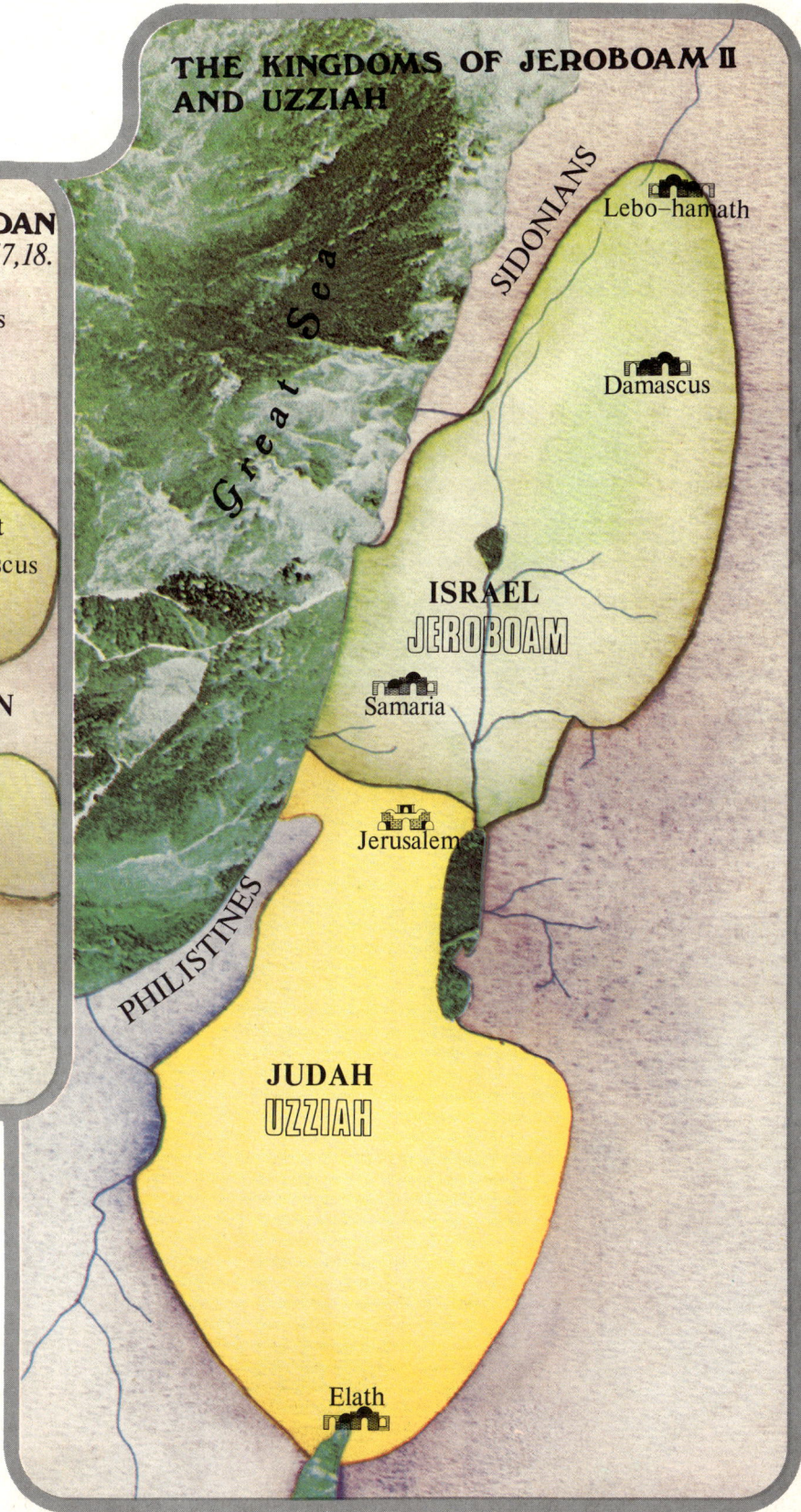

However, Amos ended his prophecies with hope for the future when the Jewish people would return to their land and the dynasty of King David would be restored to its former splendour.

Hosea who had witnessed the terrible events which occurred in his native Kingdom of Israel denounced the treacherous conduct of the society in the southern Kingdom and prophesied captivity and destruction of the Kingdom. In his warnings to the people he showed compassion and feeling for a society that lacked knowledge of the ways and nature of God. He too foretold an era when Israel would change its ways and repent, and God in turn would forgive His people and return them to the land of their fathers.

Hoshea was the last king of Israel, and during his reign there were population exchanges in the whole area. Through this movement of people emerged the Samaritans, a tiny remnant of which survives to the present time. It was the political intrigues and revolutions which brought about Israel's downfall.

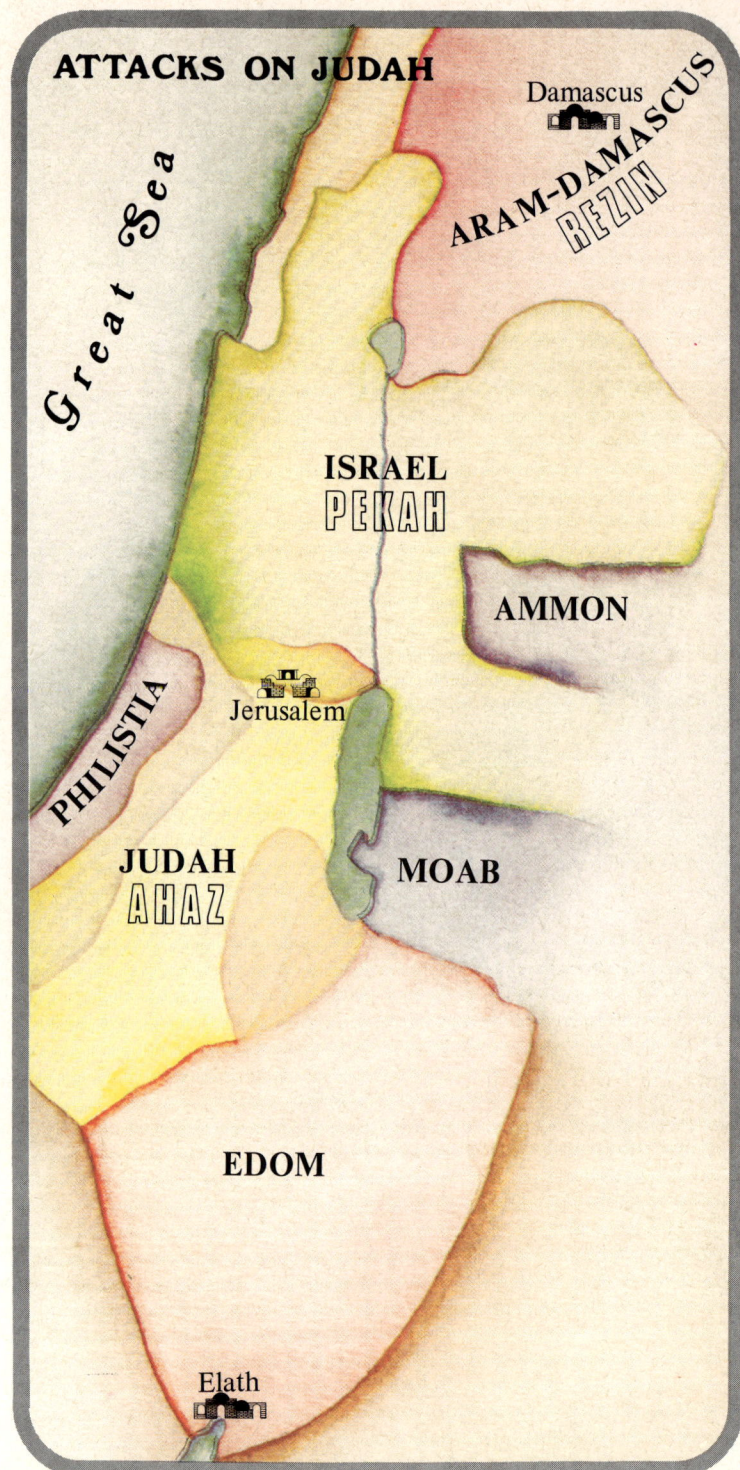

**ATTACKS ON JUDAH**

| | |
|---|---|
| Fall of Northern Kingdom | 722 BCE |
| Jeremiah (prophetic) | 626 BCE |
| Josiah | 638-609 BCE |
| Capture of Jerusalem by Babylonians | 597 BCE |
| Ezekial (prophetic) | 592 BCE |
| First destruction of the Temple | 586 BCE |
| First return of Babylonian Exiles | 537 BCE |
| Ezra & second return of Babylonian Exiles | 458 BCE |
| Maccabean Uprising | 167 BCE |
| Destruction of the Second Temple | 70 CE |

# THE FALL OF ISRAEL

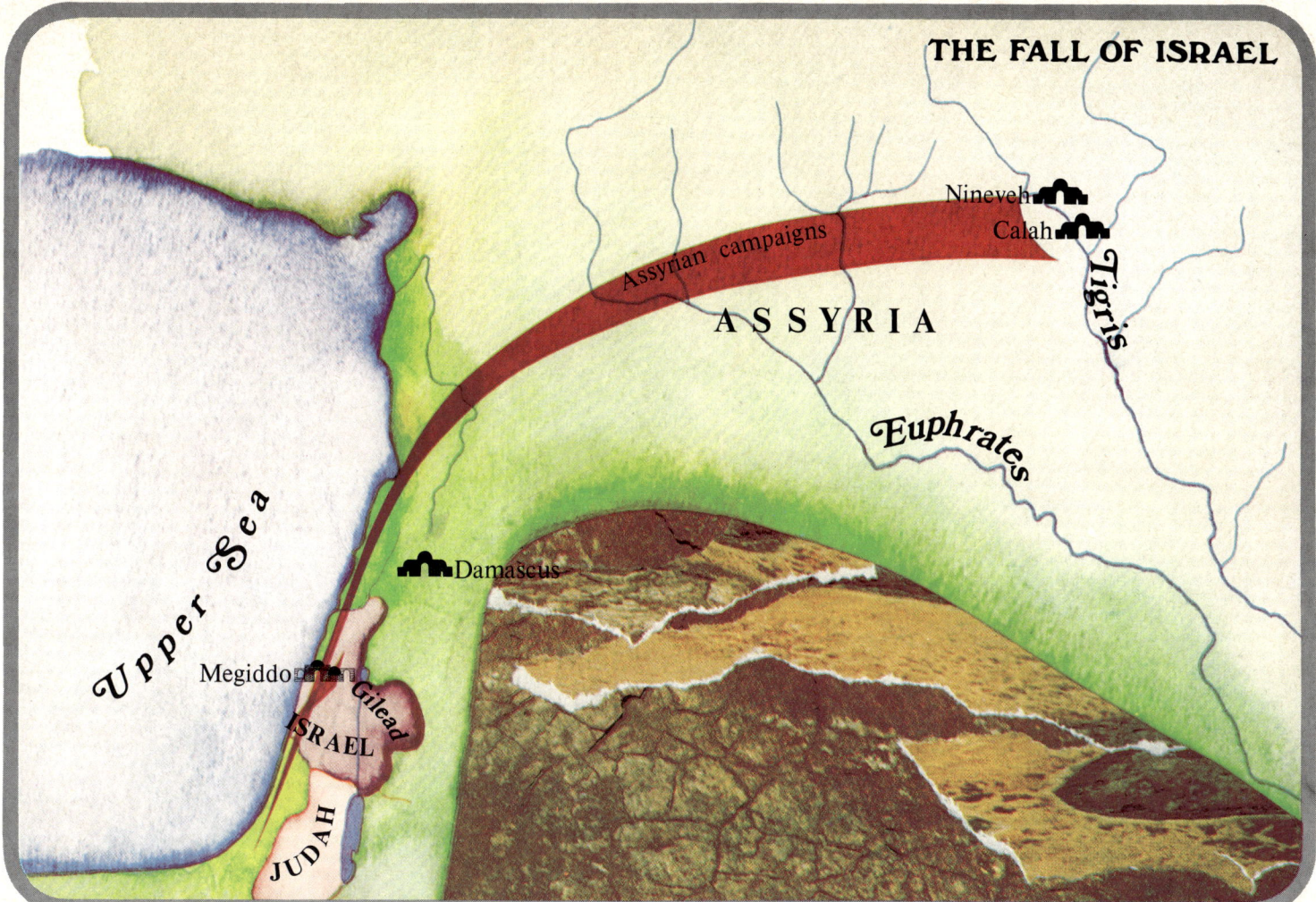

Nineveh
Calah
*Tigris*
Assyrian campaigns
A S S Y R I A
*Euphrates*
*Upper Sea*
Damascus
Megiddo
Gilead
ISRAEL
JUDAH

# POPULATION EXCHANGES UNDER TIGLATH-PILESER III

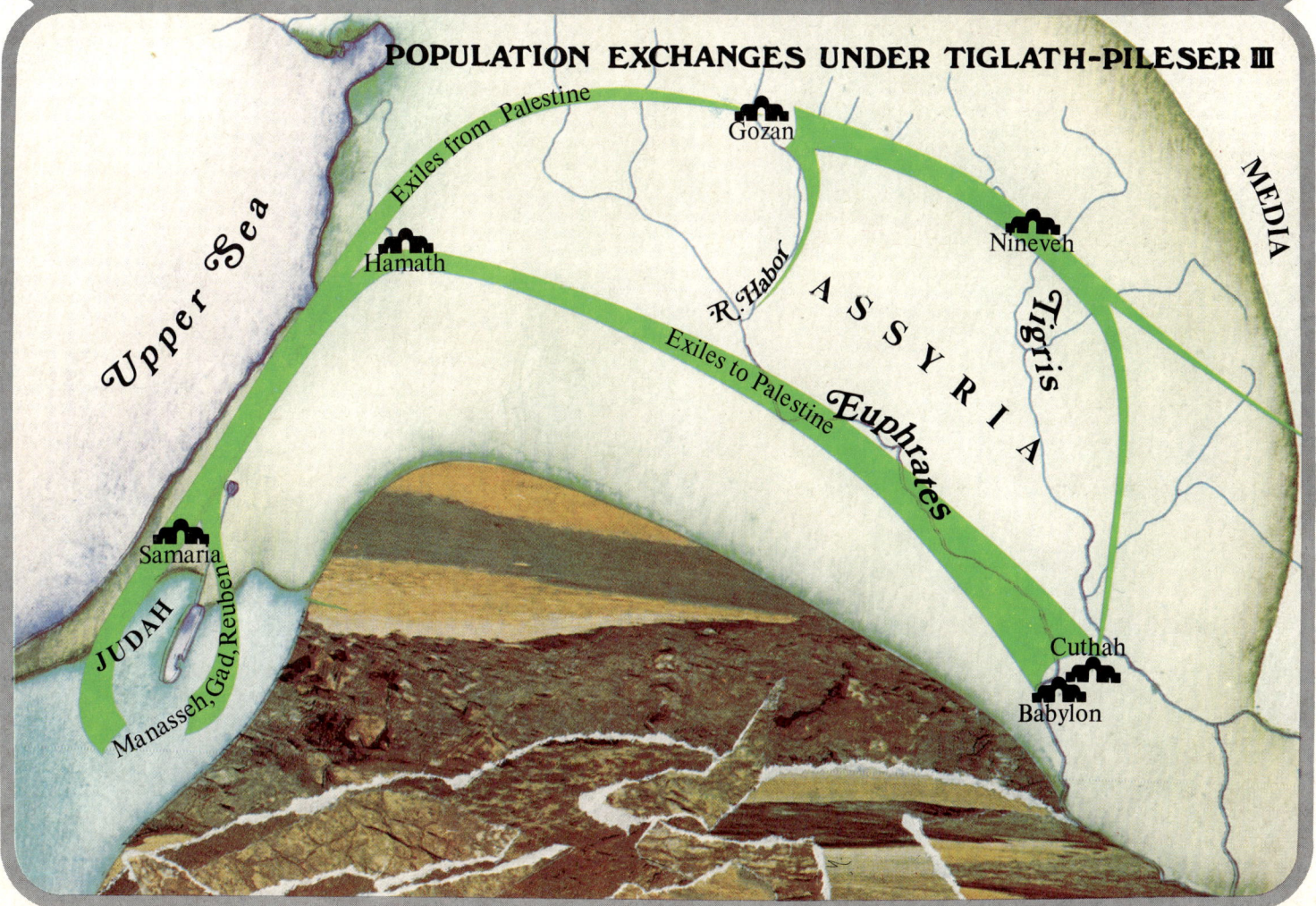

Exiles from Palestine
Gozan
MEDIA
Hamath
Nineveh
R. Habol
A S S Y R I A
*Tigris*
Exiles to Palestine
*Euphrates*
*Upper Sea*
Samaria
JUDAH
Manasseh, Gad, Reuben
Cuthah
Babylon

# THE FALL OF JUDAH

*(II Kings 22-25)*

721-587 BCE

The end of the northern kingdom of Israel saw over 27,000 captives taken to the cities of the Medes, but the kingdom of Judah continued as a self-governing monarchy, and after the death of king Ahaz his son Hezekiah succeeded him. This new king was a pious and God-fearing man who abolished the idols which his father Ahaz had brought into the Temple worship. The king's wish to destroy every kind of idol was soon followed by the Judeans breaking down all idolatrous altars, and for the first time since the days of Solomon the Temple became again the only place for worship to God in the whole of Judah.

At that time there lived the prophet Isaiah who was pleased to see the changes which the king and the people had made. However, the prophet was not entirely satisfied with the situation as some of the nobles were not interested in religion and spent their time asking the king to consider an alliance with Egypt in order to rebel against Assyria. Other countries in the region were prepared to join in the revolt and Isaiah, who warned the Judeans against such action, could not persuade the king to ignore the wrong advice given him by the nobles.

The death of the Assyrian king was followed by his son Sennacherib taking over his father's plans for the expansion of the Assyrian Empire. Hezekiah could foresee that sooner or later Assyria would attack Judah and Jerusalem, so he improved the essential water supply of Jerusalem by digging a tunnel which became known as the Siloam Tunnel or Canal, to bring water from the Kidron Valley to the south of Jerusalem. To this day water flows through this tunnel, and a party of explorers in 1880 came across inscriptions in the

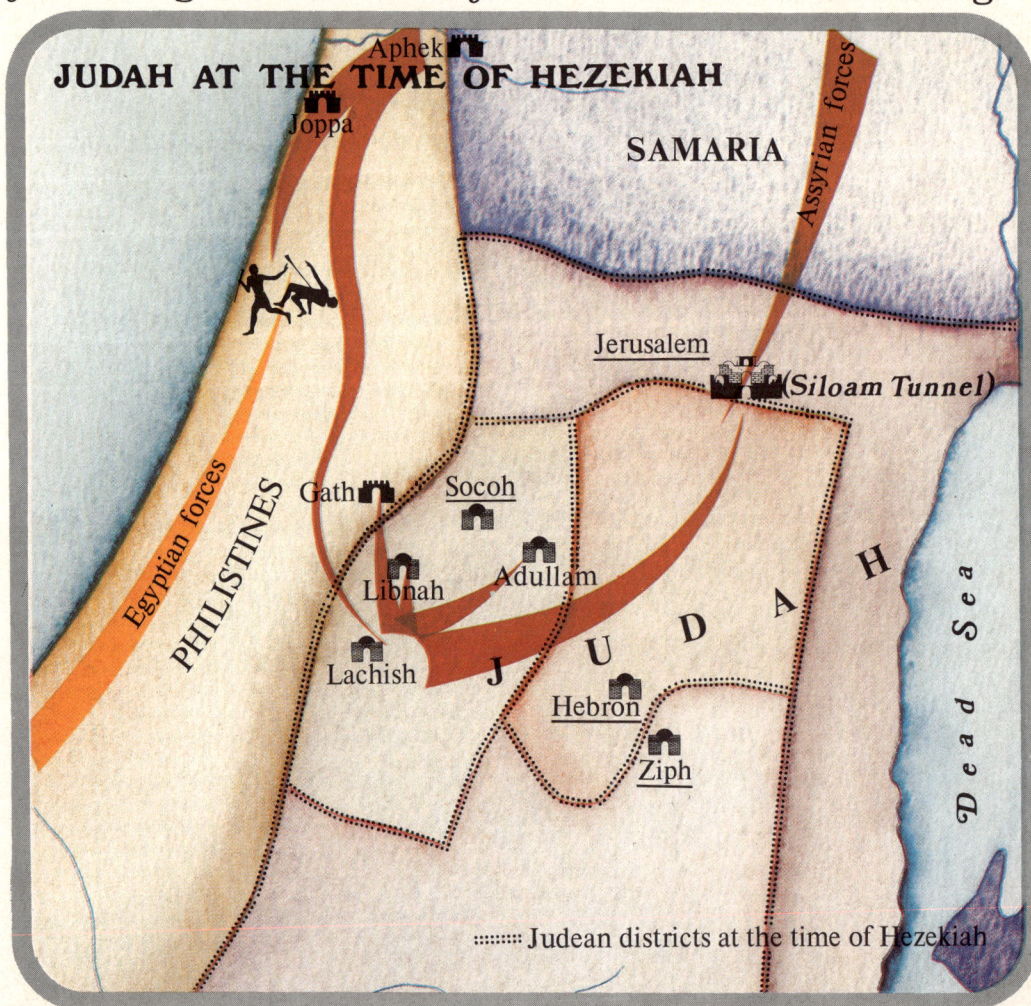

JUDAH AT THE TIME OF HEZEKIAH

Aphek
Joppa
SAMARIA
Assyrian forces
Jerusalem
(Siloam Tunnel)
Egyptian forces
PHILISTINES
Gath
Socoh
Libnah
Adullam
Lachish
J U D A H
Hebron
Ziph
Dead Sea

⠿⠿⠿ Judean districts at the time of Hezekiah

Carchemish
605 BCE

Haran

ASSYRIAN

Nineveh
612 BCE

MEDIA

EMPIRE

Great Sea

Assyrian empire at its greatest extent

Babylonians

Babylon

Megiddo
609 BCE

JUDAH

Josiah's kingdom

NECHO

EGYPT

tunnel which describe how workmen began to dig the tunnel from opposite ends. When they were five feet apart they heard each other's voices and realised that completion of the tunnel was at hand.

It was not long before Sennacherib fought and crushed Judah's allies and then decided to deal with Judah by taking many fortified cities including Lachish. In the British Museum, London, can be seen a model of the siege and capture of Lachish which was on display in Sennacherib's palace at Nineveh. It was at Lachish that king Hezekiah of Judah surrendered, and Sennacherib demanded heavy taxes from the king.

Soon Sennacherib wanted to capture Jerusalem itself, the very heart of Judea, but he was forestalled by the news that an Egyptian army was marching against him. Sennacherib changed his plans and sent a letter to Hezekiah demanding complete surrender. Hezekiah went to the Temple with the letter, which he spread out before God, and he prayed. The prophet Isaiah brought him the answer to his pleas and prayers. He told the king that the Assyrian king would never capture Jerusalem. That same night the Assyrian forces lost many thousands of soldiers as a result of a plague and Sennacherib himself quickly returned to Assyria only to be killed by his two sons.

King Hezekiah's reign ended peacefully and in prosperity. On his death he was succeeded by his son Manasseh who was only 12 years old and for a time it was really the nobles who ruled the country. As Manasseh grew to man-

MEDIAN EMPIRE

ASSYRIA

R. Euphrates

R. Tigris

ELAM

Great Sea

Babylon

BABYLONIAN EMPIRE

EGYPT

Lower Sea

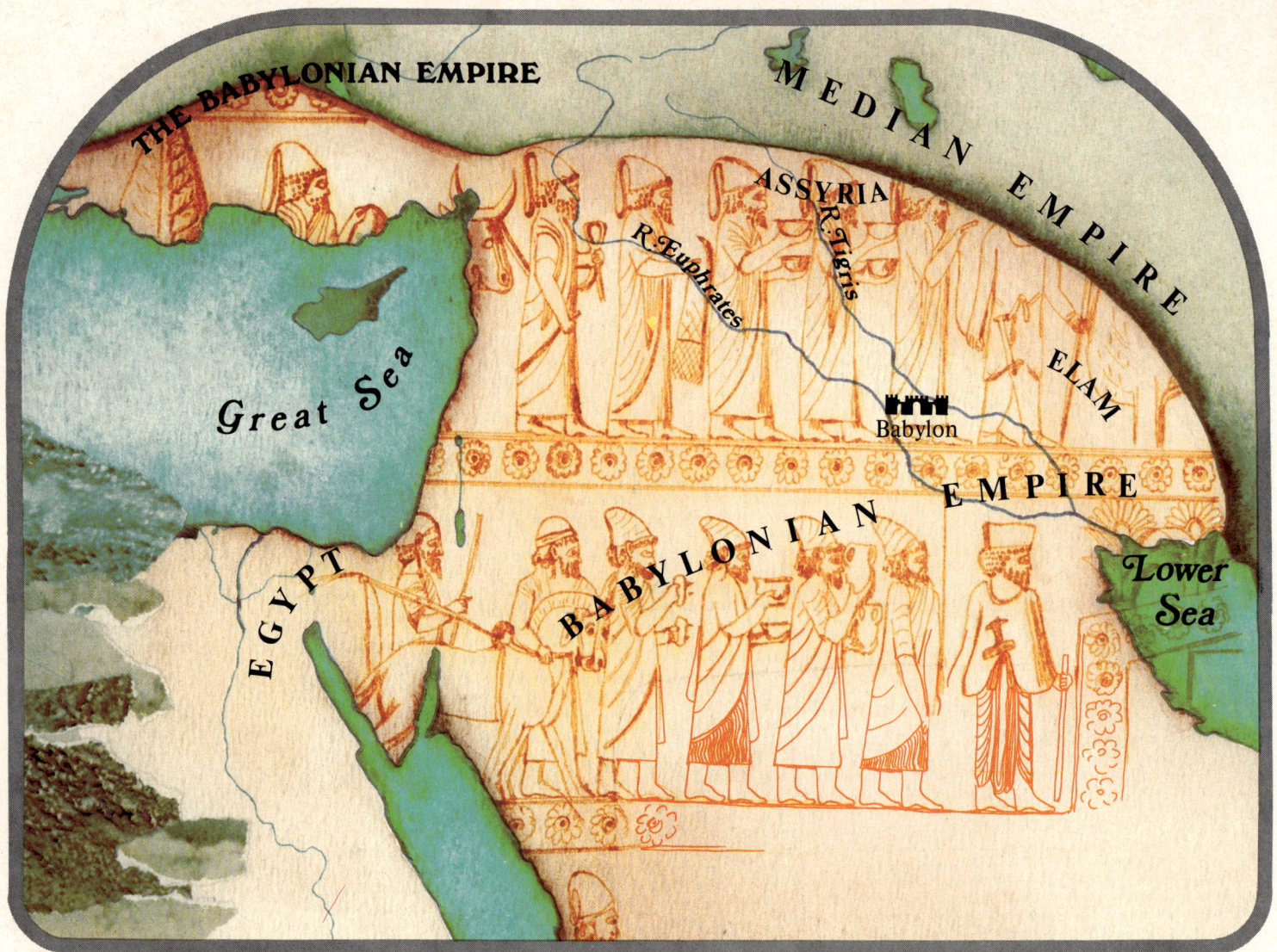

hood he was constantly guided in the wrong way and during his 55 year reign over Judah he undid all the good deeds of his father, King Hezekiah. The prophet Isaiah spoke out against all the actions of king Manasseh but his words were rejected and scorned, Judah seemed like any other province of Assyria.

When king Manasseh died, his son ruled for two years and then the young boy of eight, Josiah, became king. When he was 20 years old, Assyria began to collapse, and Josiah listened to the words of the prophets Nahum and Zephania. He swept away the idols, altars and images in Jerusalem and the cities of Judah, and even turned to the former northern kingdom of Israel to destroy the heathen altars and idols.

With the fall of the Assyrian Empire it was left to the armies of Egypt and Babylon to decide on mastery of the area. The prophet Jeremiah had warned the Judeans for 23 years that the Babylonians would come and take Judah into captivity if the people did not alter their bad ways and follow the commands of God. At a great battle at Carchemish on the Euphrates, the Babylonians defeated the Egyptians and Nebuchadnezzar, king of Babylon, became the master of the former Assyrian Empire.

After a siege of 18 months Jerusalem, together with the Temple, was captured and destroyed and the last king of Judah, Zedekiah, was blinded and taken into captivity to Babylon together with thousands of Jews. So began the Babylonian Exile.

# THE CAPTIVITY IN BABYLON

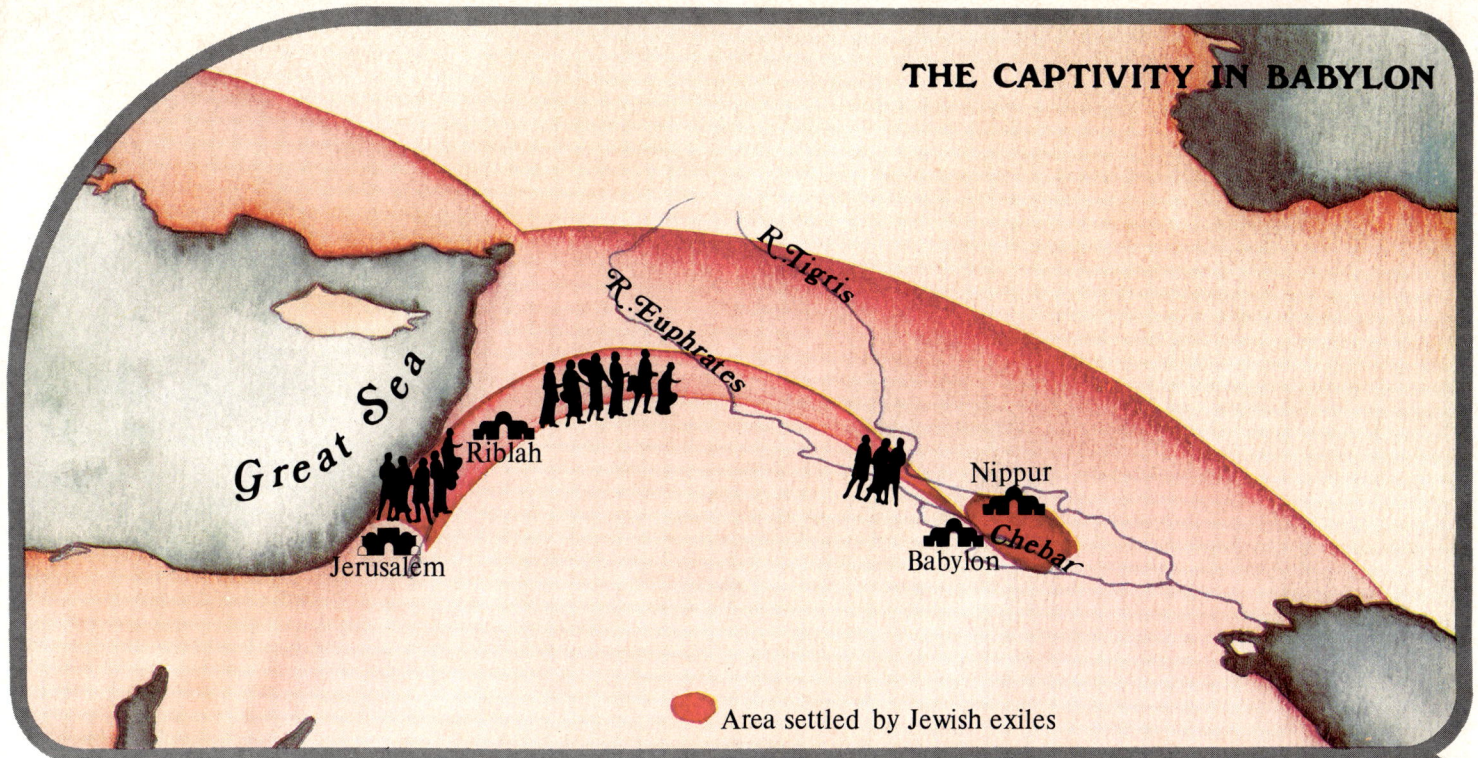

Great Sea

R. Tigris

R. Euphrates

Riblah

Jerusalem

Nippur

Chebar

Babylon

Area settled by Jewish exiles

# JUDAH AFTER THE EXILE

Area inhabited by Jews before the exile
Concentrations of Jewish inhabitants after the exile

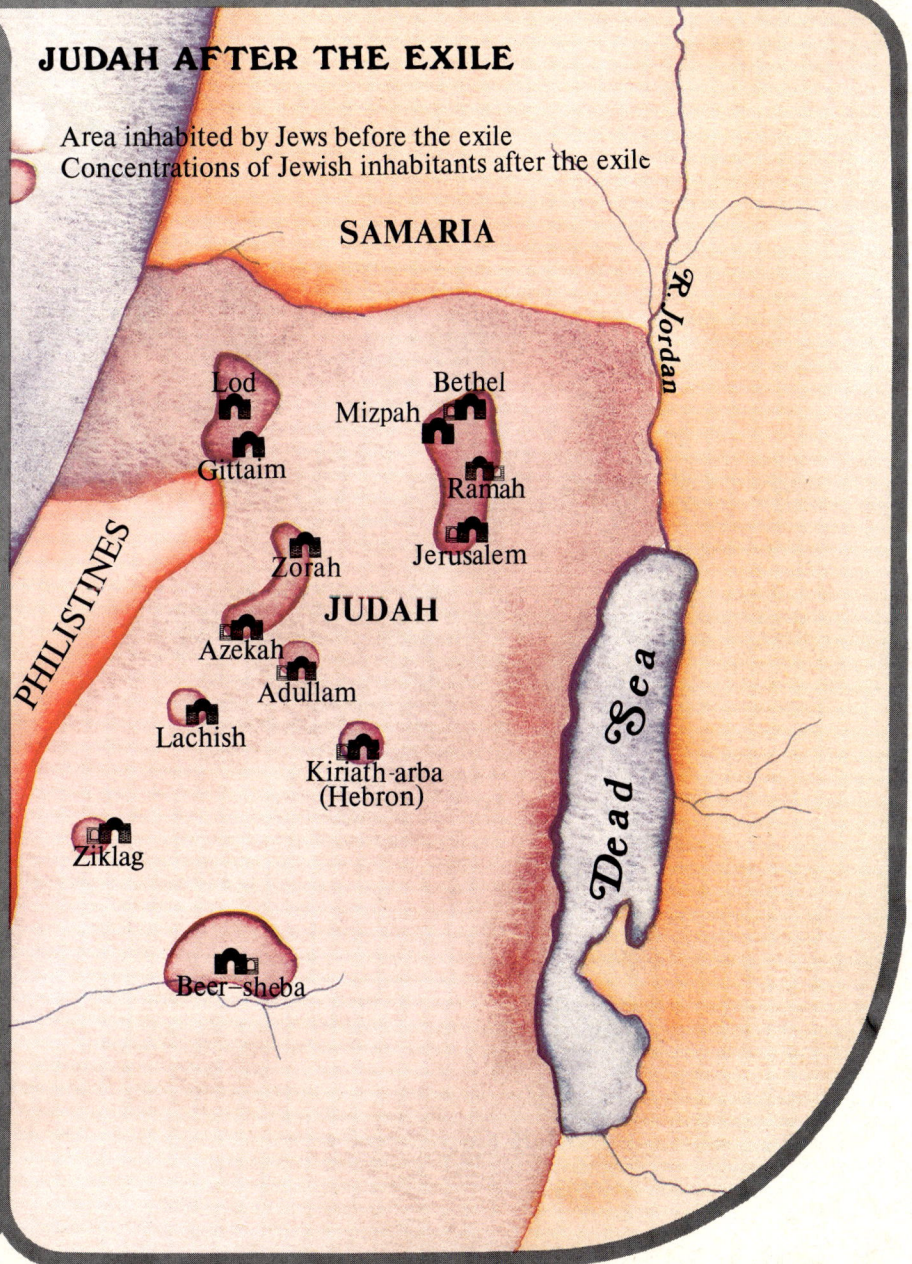

SAMARIA

R. Jordan

Lod

Bethel

Mizpah

Gittaim

Ramah

Jerusalem

Zorah

JUDAH

Azekah

Adullam

Lachish

Kiriath-arba
(Hebron)

Ziklag

Dead Sea

Beer-sheba

PHILISTINES

# NEBUCHADNEZZAR'S CAMPAIGNS IN JUDAH

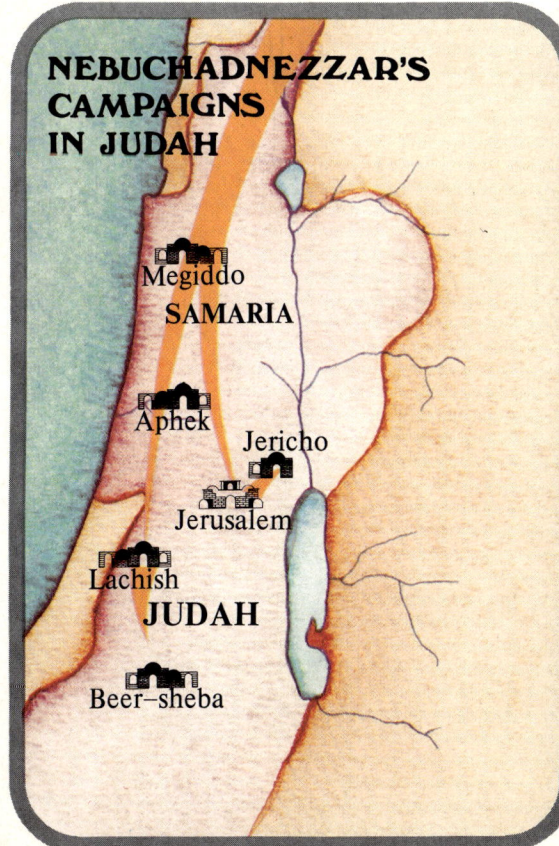

Megiddo

SAMARIA

Aphek

Jericho

Jerusalem

Lachish

JUDAH

Beer-sheba

# EXILE AND RETURN

*(Ezra 1-10; Nehemiah 1-13; Daniel; Esther)*

587-332 BCE

Amongst those led away to Babylon were the prophet Ezekiel and the wise Daniel who played an important part during the Jewish exile. Many of those who were taken captive were learned and righteous people who observed God's commandments and continued to study the Torah in their new surroundings. Ezekiel's prophecies gave hope to the exiles by proclaiming that they would return to their homeland if they returned to the ways of God. He stressed the importance of the holiness of the Sabbath and Festivals and the observance of all the commandments. The Jews were allowed to lead their own way of life and soon developed a culture which was to become the basis of Jewish learning for all future generations.

Daniel was soon promoted to a high position in the royal court. He was able to interpret the strange dreams that were troubling king Nebuchadnezzar, but at the same time Daniel and his friends remained loyal to the Jewish faith and would not do anything which was against Jewish law and custom. It was during this period that the Babylonian Empire reached its peak in power and prosperity. During a special feast for his nobles given by Belshazzar who was then king of Babylon, a mysterious message appeared on the palace walls. The king was terrified and promised great honour to anyone who could explain the meaning of the message. It was only Daniel who could interpret the four Aramaic words, which contained hidden warnings for Belshazzar. Daniel was rewarded and soon the foretold events actually happened.

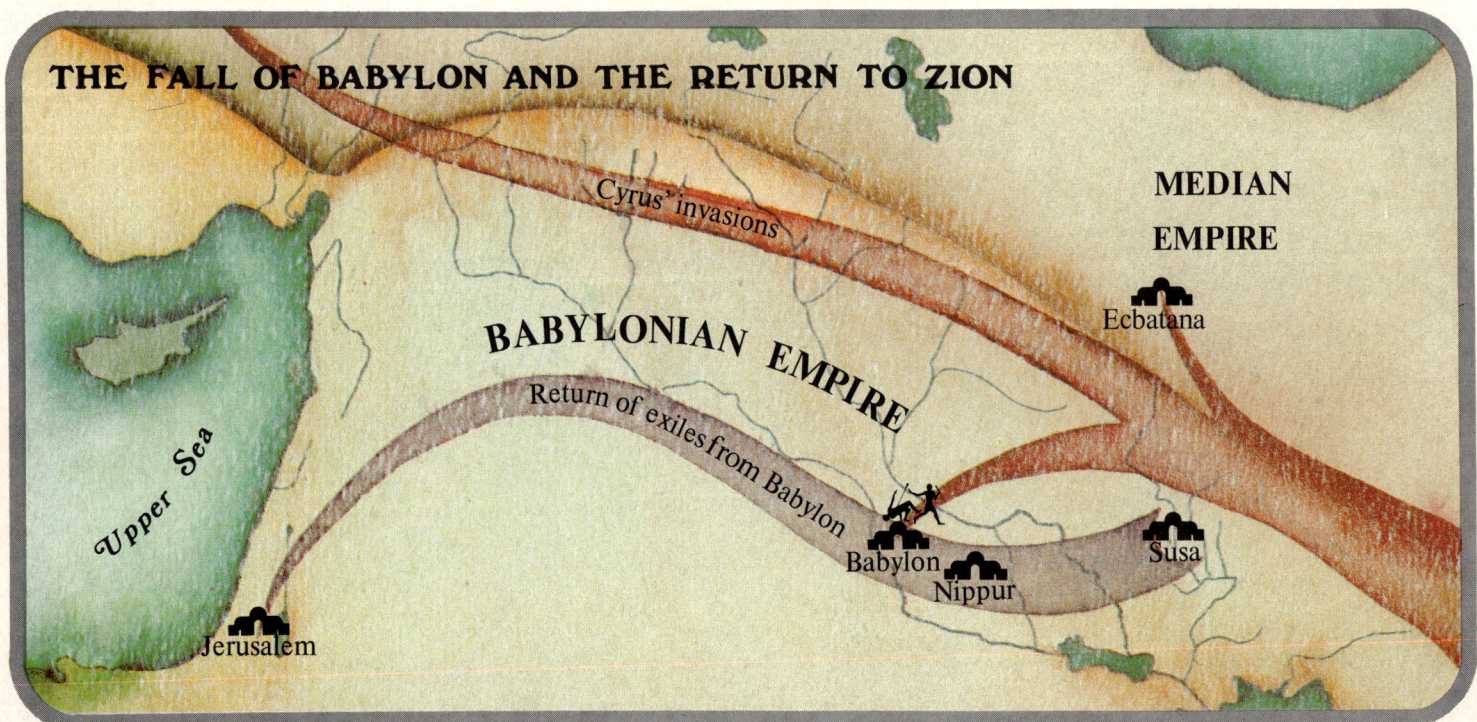

THE FALL OF BABYLON AND THE RETURN TO ZION

Cyrus' invasions

MEDIAN EMPIRE

Ecbatana

BABYLONIAN EMPIRE

Return of exiles from Babylon

Upper Sea

Babylon

Nippur

Susa

Jerusalem

The whole of the Babylonian Empire passed into the hands of Cyrus of Persia and the Jewish exiles prayed for their captivity to end. Soon after his conquest Cyrus issued a proclamation which allowed Jews to return to Zion and the land of their fathers. He also gave them permission to rebuild the Temple which Nebuchadnezzar's army had destroyed and he returned the holy vessels which the soldiers had taken to Babylon. For 50 years the Jews had been exiled from their land.

Those who returned found the land desolate and neglected. They spent much time building houses and developing the farmland which their leaders had allocated them. But their main purpose was to rebuild the Temple, and eventually the foundation stones of the Second Temple were laid with great solemnity accompanied by singing and music.

Haman, chief minister to king Ahasuerus, plotted to wipe out the Jews who were living in the Persian Empire. Through the intervention of Queen Esther, who was a Jewess, the Jews were spared and Haman and his plotters were killed instead. Jews continued to have an influence at the Persian court and a Jewish cup-bearer called Nehemiah was appointed governor of Jerusalem. Another group of exiles left Babylon for the Holy Land led by a scribe, Ezra, who renewed religious life and appointed magistrates and judges empowered to punish anyone who disobeyed the laws of God.

Ezra and Nehemiah had established the teachings of the Torah as the authority governing the lives of the Jews and they were to prove the main source of the preservation of the Jewish people throughout their future history and destiny.

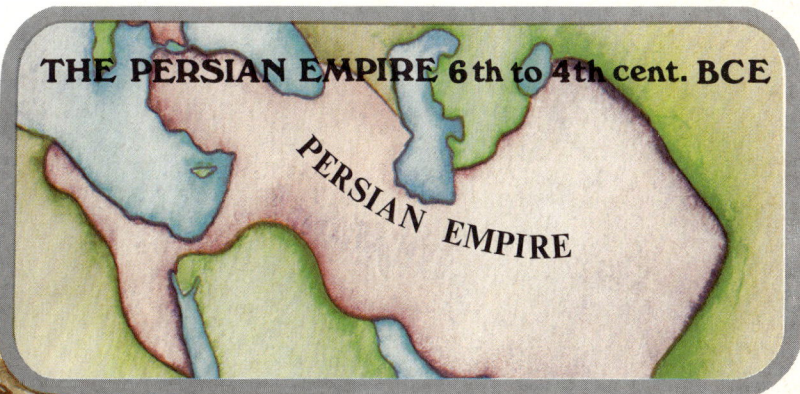

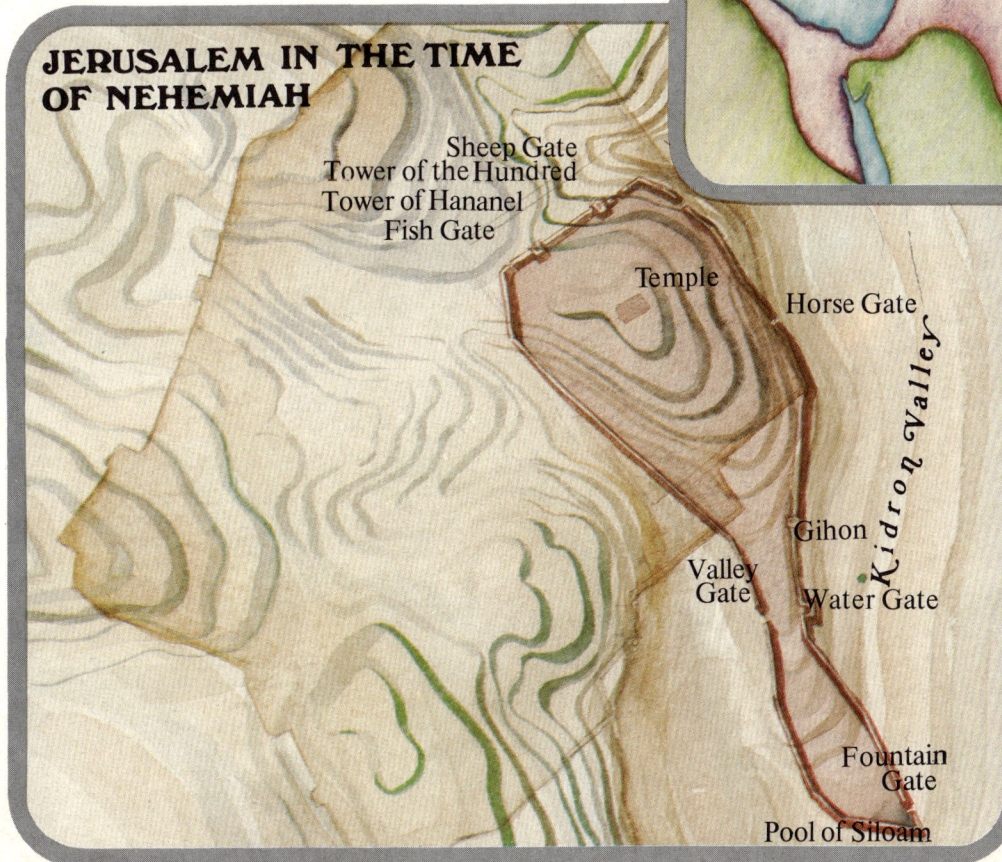

**THE PERSIAN EMPIRE 6th to 4th cent. BCE**

PERSIAN EMPIRE

**JERUSALEM IN THE TIME OF NEHEMIAH**

Sheep Gate
Tower of the Hundred
Tower of Hananel
Fish Gate

Temple

Horse Gate

Kidron Valley

Gihon

Valley Gate

Water Gate

Fountain Gate

Pool of Siloam

### SECOND TEMPLE
**537 BCE**
Foundation stone laid. Work stopped for 16 years.

**516 BCE**
Completed — 70 years after Destruction of First Temple.

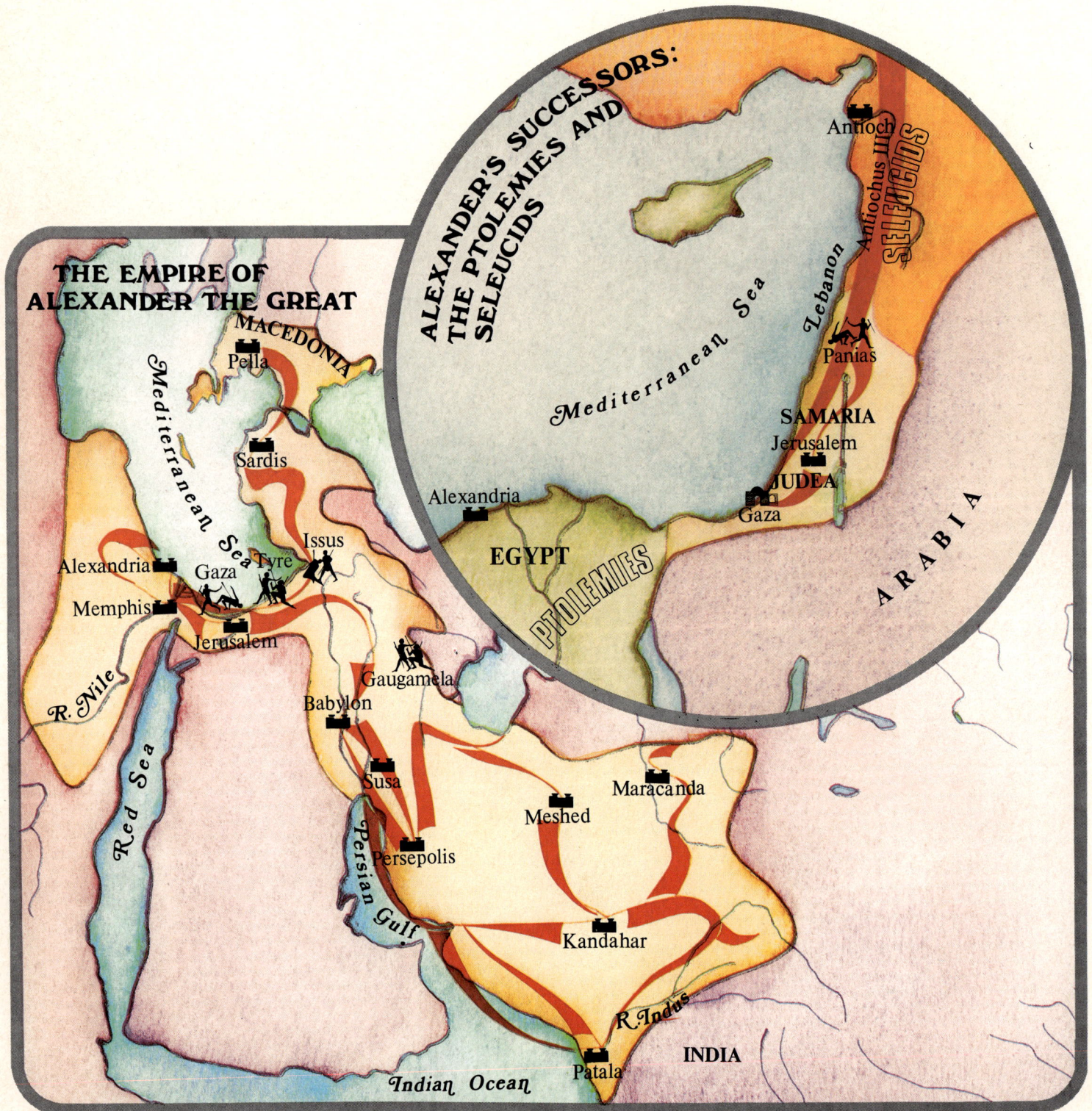

# THE RULE OF GREECE

*(Daniel 11:3-30; I Maccabees 1)*
332-167 BCE

**THE EMPIRE OF ALEXANDER THE GREAT**

*Mediterranean Sea*

MACEDONIA
Pella
Sardis
Issus
Tyre
Gaza
Alexandria
Memphis
Jerusalem
*R. Nile*
*Red Sea*
Gaugamela
Babylon
Susa
*Persian Gulf*
Persepolis
Meshed
Maracanda
Kandahar
*R. Indus*
Patala
**INDIA**
*Indian Ocean*

ALEXANDER'S SUCCESSORS: THE PTOLEMIES AND SELEUCIDS

Antioch
Antiochus III
SELEUCIDS
*Mediterranean Sea*
*Lebanon*
Panias
SAMARIA
Jerusalem
JUDEA
Gaza
Alexandria
EGYPT
PTOLEMIES
ARABIA

58

The time of the religious revival, which was led by Ezra and Nehemiah, was comparatively peaceful. The Persian conquerors were constantly busy with their Greek wars and it became possible for groups of exiles to leave Syria and return to Judea or to form a new Jewish community in Egypt. Scholars were able to concentrate on their work and produce important writings which were to remain for all time as authoritative works on Jewish law, ethics, ritual, morals and prayer.

After more than 200 years the powerful Persian Empire was defeated. Alexander of Macedonia led his strong army into Asia and was victorious in his battles, conquering vast areas in the region including Syria, Samaria and Judea, as well as Egypt where the city of Alexandria was founded. Many Jews were amongst the early settlers of this new city, who were influenced by Greek culture and thought and neglected their own national language of Hebrew. They built a very large and beautiful synagogue which was of such a size that the voice of the Cantor could not be heard by all worshippers, and flags had to be waved as signals for saying the responses.

After his Egyptian conquest Alexander crossed the rivers Euphrates and Tigris and defeated the Persians overthrowing the whole Persian Empire. However, when Alexander had added other countries to his empire and decided that it was time to put a halt to wars and conquests and return home, he became ill in Babylon and died of a fever. Immediately Alexander's generals divided the great conquests amongst themselves, and the Holy Land became the area between the two rival powers of Egypt and Syria. At the beginning Egypt had the upper hand and was ruled by the Ptolemies whereas the Syrians were ruled by the Seleucids. The Jews of the Holy Land had a Ptolemaic governor and paid their taxes to Egypt with the priests running the country, and religious activity very much as before.

It was not long before Syria, ruled by Antiochus III, a king of the Seleucid dynasty, became more ambitious and captured the Holy Land from Egypt. Although the Jews had a change of masters, their position remained the same as far as local government was concerned. So it remained for some years, but as the Syrian civilisation was Greek in its culture and way of worship the Syrians came to despise the Jewish way of life and waited for an opportunity to destroy Jewish observances and beliefs.

Over the years the government of the Jews was in the hands of the High Priest. Ezra had established the important body known as "The Men of the Great Assembly" who were all men of stature to whom the people listened and respected. But trouble began when Onias III was High Priest and he called on the Syrians to settle a family dispute. This was the opportune moment for which king Antiochus had been waiting. The Jewish leaders had begun to quarrel and riot amongst themselves and the disunity encouraged

Antiochus to take action which would destroy everything which the Jews valued. He entered Jerusalem, robbed the Temple of its ritual objects and desecrated it by placing swine's flesh on the altar. Many of the inhabitants were killed and he tried to abolish the Jewish religion. The sacred scriptures of the Jews were burned and the Reading of the Torah was forbidden on pain of death. Great rewards were offered to those who would renounce Judaism altogether.

Many heroic stories are related during that period of Jewish history and the martyrs who remained steadfast to the covenant which the Jewish people had made with God at Sinai outnumbered those who were weak and yielded to the persecutors. It was at this time that both the weak and the strong felt strong resentment about what was going on and waited for some kind of leadership to give expression to their feeling in a practical manner. This came about when an elderly priest called Mattathias from the small town of Modi'in, not far from Jerusalem, refused to obey the commands of an officer of Antiochus, and gathered around him his sons and Jews who were prepared to revolt against the Seleucid Kingdom. Mattathias and his followers began a battle which was to last for 27 years, resulting in a victory for the Jews. When Mattathias died his son Judah, known as the Maccabee, took over the leadership of the rebels.

Those who fought were, in the main, religious Jews, men who were prepared to give up their lives for the ways of the Torah and for the Holy Land. For this reason it became the custom of the chief general of Antiochus to attack the Jews on the Sabbath, believing that because of their strong religious observance of the Torah laws they would not defend themselves. He was not aware that rulings had been made which permitted the Jews if attacked to fight and defend themselves for their land or their faith on the Sabbath as bravely as on a week-day.

At the end of many years of battle, Judah the Maccabee marched with his troops into Jerusalem and liberated the Temple. It was cleansed, purified and re-dedicated on the 25th of the Hebrew month of Kislev and its anniversary was instituted as a religious and historical observance amongst Jews ever since by the lighting of candles for eight days.

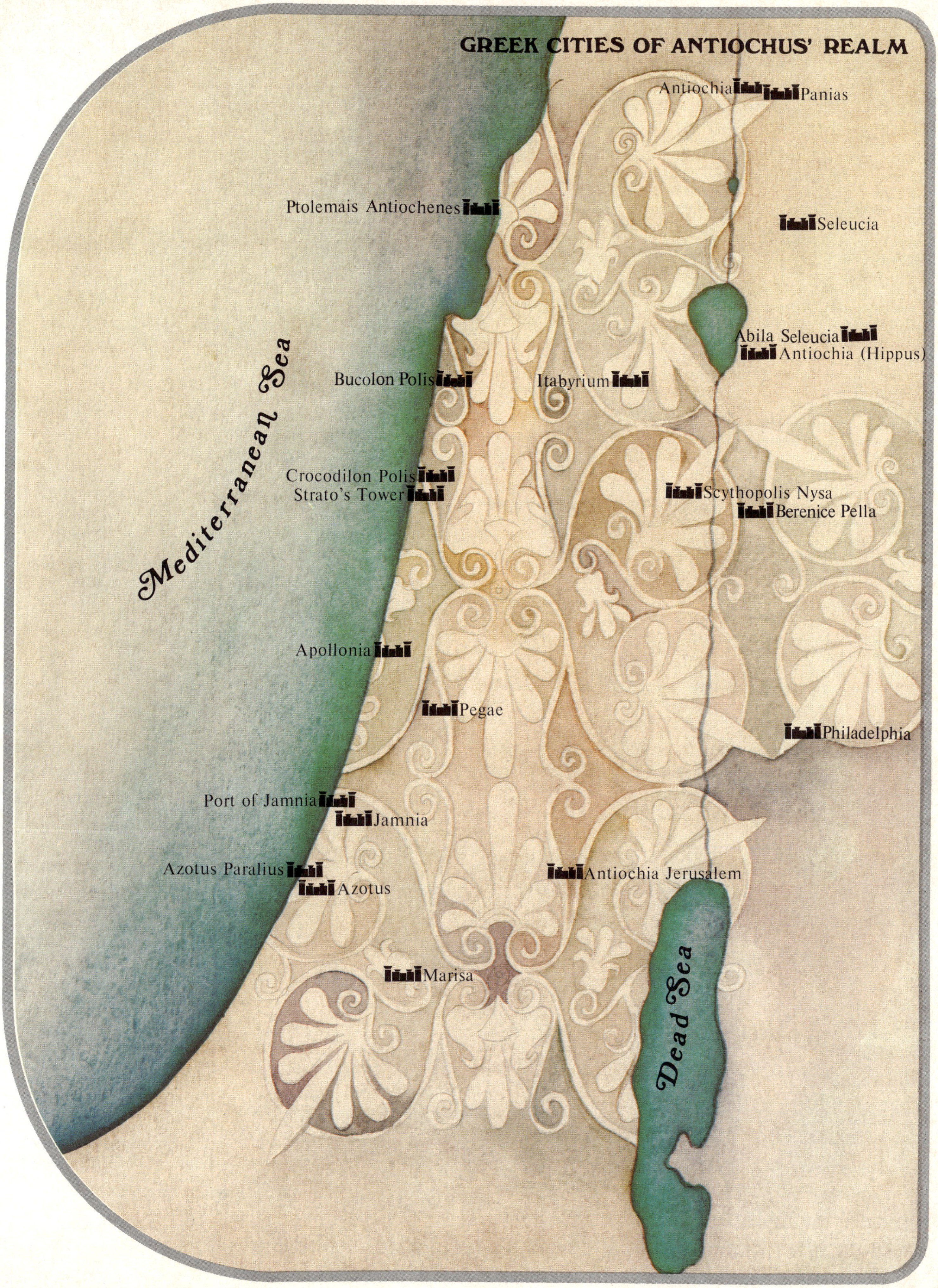

GREEK CITIES OF ANTIOCHUS' REALM
Antiochia
Panias
Ptolemais Antiochenes
Seleucia
Abila Seleucia
Antiochia (Hippus)
Bucolon Polis
Itabyrium
Mediterranean Sea
Crocodilon Polis
Strato's Tower
Scythopolis Nysa
Berenice Pella
Apollonia
Pegae
Philadelphia
Port of Jamnia
Jamnia
Azotus Paralius
Azotus
Antiochia Jerusalem
Marisa
Dead Sea

JUDAS' CAMPAIGNS OUTSIDE
JUDEA
*1 Maccabees 5*

Ptolemais

Judas
Simon

SAMARIA

Gilead

Acrabeta
Joppa    Idumeans

Jamnia         Jazer
Azotus    JUDEA    Timotheus

Marisa   Jerusalem   Baal-meon
Beonites

Hebron
IDUMEA

# THE MACCABEES
# AND THE
# HASMONEAN DYNASTY

*(I Maccabees 2-16)*
167-63 BCE

J udas Maccabeus was now concerned with the military security of the Maccabean position around Jerusalem. He began by strengthening the southern approach to Jerusalem in Beth-zur and then turned his attention to the Jews

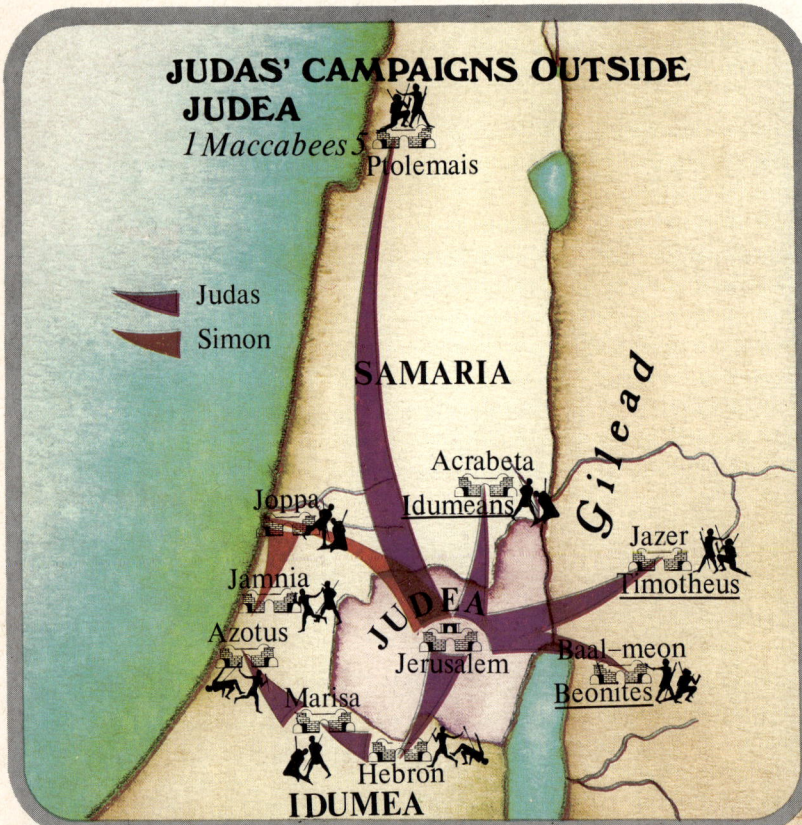

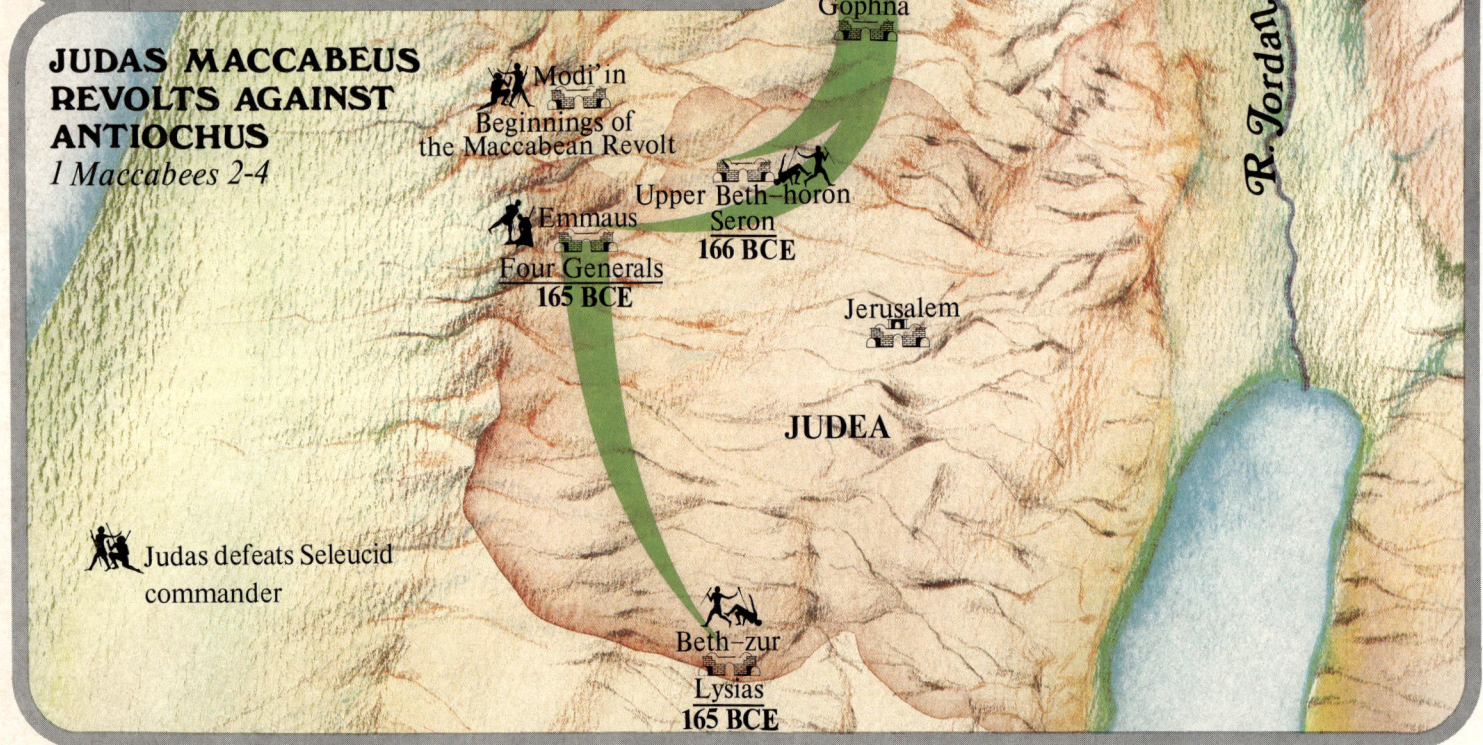

JUDAS MACCABEUS
REVOLTS AGAINST
ANTIOCHUS
*1 Maccabees 2-4*

Apollonius
167 BCE

Gophna Hills

R. Jordan

Gophna

Modi'in
Beginnings of
the Maccabean Revolt

Upper Beth-horon
Emmaus    Seron
Four Generals    166 BCE
165 BCE

Jerusalem

JUDEA

Judas defeats Seleucid
commander

Beth-zur
Lysias
165 BCE

living just outside Judea who had appealed to Judas Maccabeus for help in their harassment by the Seleucid commanders. A rescue operation was undertaken to save Jews in places like Ptolemais (Acre), Jazer in Gilead, Joppa (Jaffa) and Azotus (Ashdod). In the meantime, Judah's brothers Simon and Jonathan were in command of troops who advanced in many directions in order to save Jews who were under dire pressure and bring them back to Judea.

Whilst the Maccabean brothers Judah, Jonathan and Simon were away on their various campaigns, two senior commanders called Azariah and Joseph were left in charge of the Jerusalem area. They wanted to repeat the successes of their leaders and struck out against the coastal city of Jamnia to prevent the Seleucid forces attacking Judea.

Judah returned to Jerusalem after his campaign in the north and attended to the Idumeans (Edomites) who occupied the Hebron hill region in the south, after the fall of Jerusalem. A sharp attack against the foes of the Jews realised the successful capture of Hebron and thereby also saved many small Jewish communities in the whole of that region. It was during these battles that Judas Maccabeus was killed, in the year 160 BCE, and he was succeeded as leader of the Maccabees by his brother Jonathan who also became High Priest. Various groups of Jews were not altogether in agreement with the leadership of the Hasmoneans and formed their own secluded communities.

These groups were mainly those who became faithful followers of the God-given law, the Torah, and who resisted the inroads of Greek culture, known as Hellenism, into the Jewish way of life and culture. Their way of life has become more familiar to us since the finding of the recently discovered Dead Sea Scrolls in Qumran which describes the small and exclusive Essene sect. They moved away from what they felt was the corruption of the cities into a remote part of the Judean Desert near the Dead Sea. They supported themselves by manual labour in the form of farming and lived together as a group by holding everything in community ownership. They were believers in personal piety and were very strict in the observance of the Torah commandments.

Other sects living at this time included the Chassidim, the Pharisees, the Sadducees and the Zealots. It was during this period that the Romans put thousands of those Jews who opposed them to death by their standard method of punishment known as crucifixion.

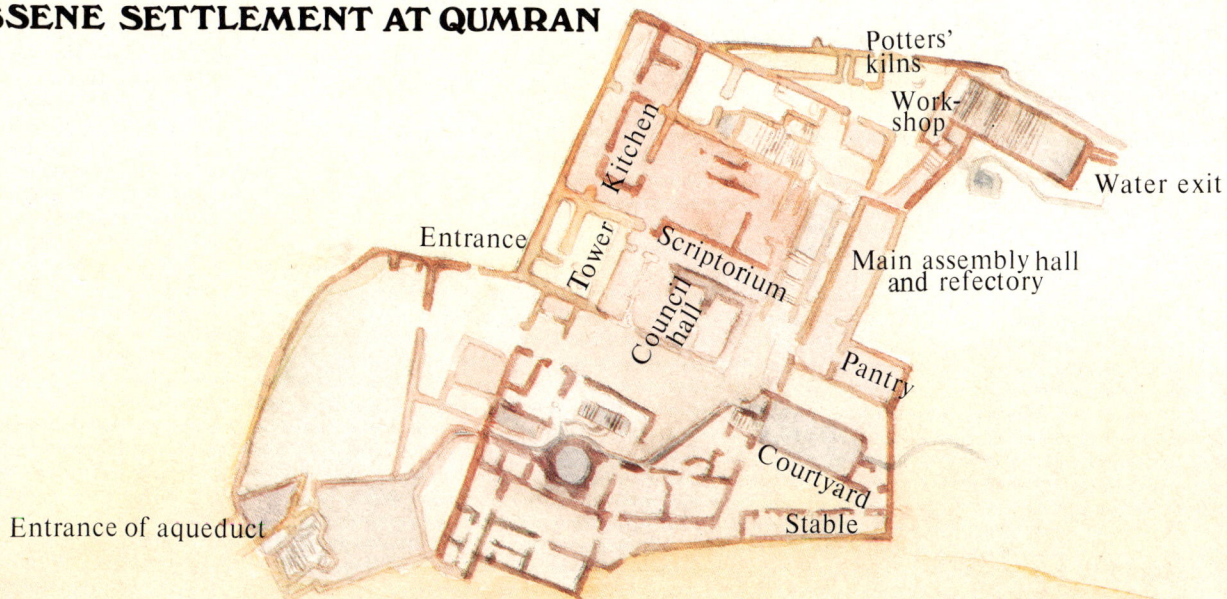

ESSENE SETTLEMENT AT QUMRAN

The Hasmonean family continued to rule the Judean region and it was during the reign of Alexander Janneus (Yannai) that the state reached the height of its power. But internally there was trouble between the Hasmonean rulers and the various sections of the people. Yannai came into open conflict with the rival factions and it was not until after his death, when his wife Salome Alexandra ruled the country, that peace finally came to the area. The Hasmoneans had a desire to expand so that they should have peace in Judea. Jonathan and Simon, Hyrcanus and Aristobulus all conquered land around Judea and Alexander Janneus's conquests created a small empire during the 27 years of his rule which took in practically the whole biblical Land of Israel (Eretz Yisrael).

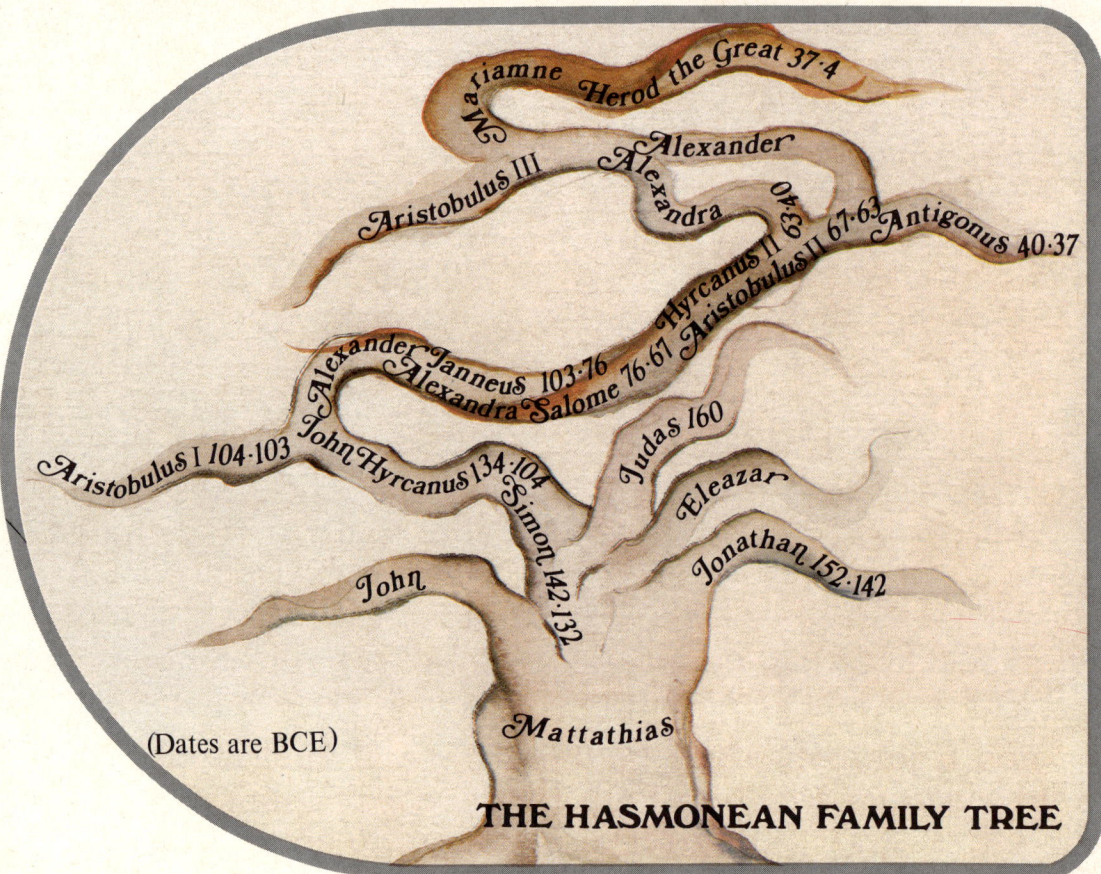

(Dates are BCE)

**THE HASMONEAN FAMILY TREE**

As Salome Alexandra was unable to be either the commander of the army or the High Priest because she was a woman, her sons Aristobulus and Hyrcanus took over these duties. She took the advice given to her when her husband was dying to form a government with the Pharisees rather than with the Sadducees. The queen's brother, Shimon ben Shetach, became the leader of the Pharisees. It proved to be a clever decision as the Pharisees were not only loyal to the commandments of the Torah, but also wise counsellors and staunch friends of Salome Alexandra. It was during the nine years of her rule of Judea that the country was both prosperous and at peace.

But it was not long before discord once again became the cause of unrest as a result of disagreement between the queen's two sons. They had different interests and after Salome Alexandra's death the two brothers began to fight for the crown. The Pharisees were on the side of Hyrcanus, who was the High Priest and elder of the two brothers, whilst the Sadducees were in favour of Aristobulus who was in charge of the army.

The bitterness between the two brothers became so great that Aristobulus in a rage asked the Roman Consul, Pompey, to settle the dispute between himself and his brother which was causing strife and hatred among the Judean population.

At that time Pompey was occupied with his conquests in Asia but eventually received representatives of both brothers at Damascus. Pompey was rather slow in making a decision and Aristobulus became impatient and left Damascus without waiting for Pompey's decision. The powerful Roman general thought the action of Aristobulus very disrespectful and determined to settle the situation in his own way. Pompey decided to march towards Jerusalem. After a siege lasting three months, Jerusalem fell in the year 63 BCE. Pompey declared Aristobulus a rebel and kept Hyrcanus as High Priest.

Pompey's war was against the people of Judea but not against Judaism and although the Temple was in his possession he commanded his army neither to desecrate it nor touch any of its treasures. Pompey brought the end of independence for Hasmonean Judea. This area now became part of the Roman Empire and the Jews became very much concerned for the future of their lives and their religion.

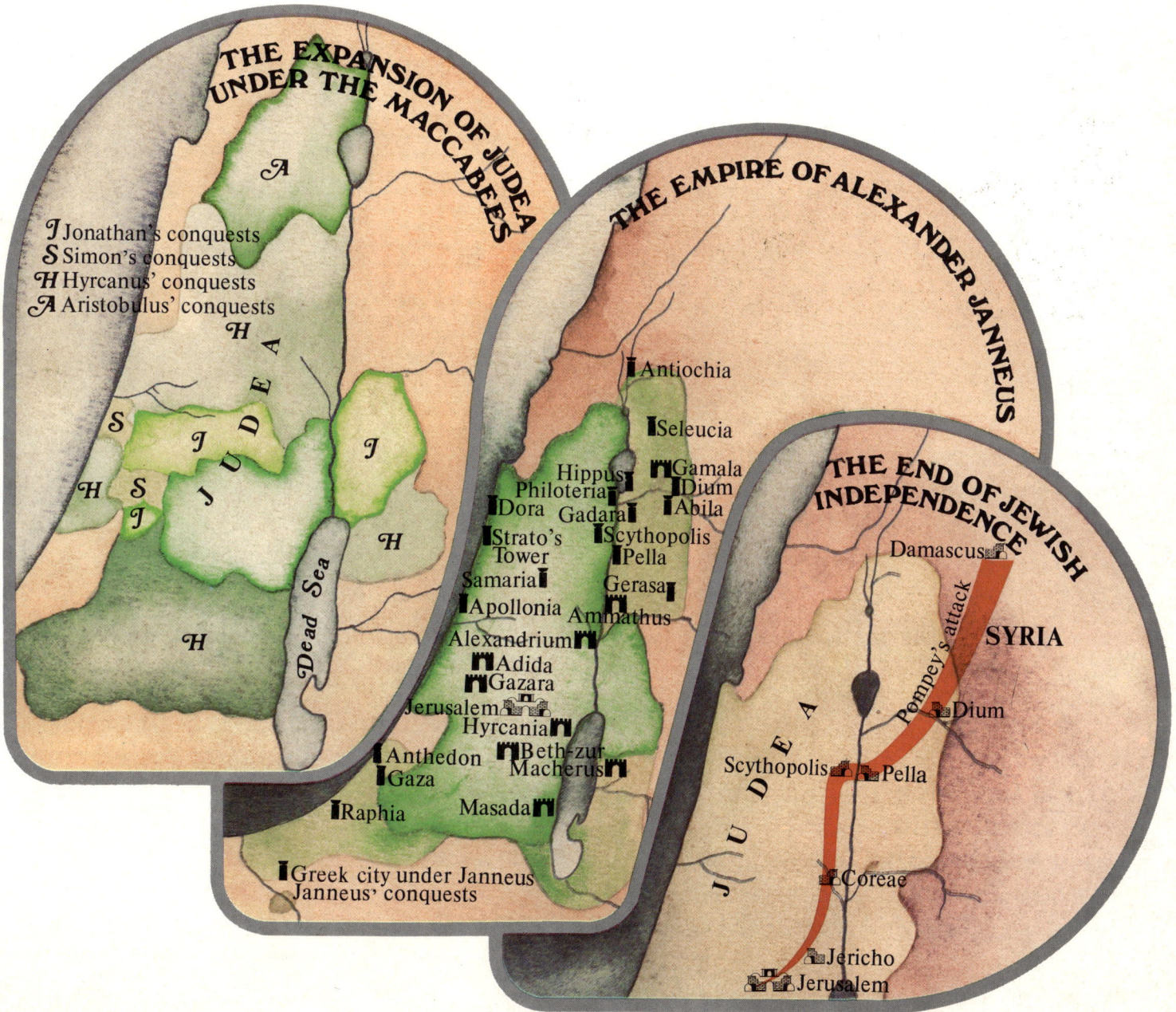

THE EXPANSION OF JUDEA UNDER THE MACCABEES

*J* Jonathan's conquests
*S* Simon's conquests
*H* Hyrcanus' conquests
*A* Aristobulus' conquests

A

H

J U D E A

S
H
S
J
J

H

H

Dead Sea

THE EMPIRE OF ALEXANDER JANNEUS

Antiochia

Seleucia

Hippus
Philoteria
Dora
Gadara
Strato's Tower
Samaria
Apollonia
Alexandrium
Adida
Gazara
Jerusalem
Hyrcania
Anthedon
Gaza
Beth-zur
Macherus
Raphia
Masada

Gamala
Dium
Abila
Scythopolis
Pella
Gerasa
Ammathus

Greek city under Janneus
Janneus' conquests

THE END OF JEWISH INDEPENDENCE

Damascus

SYRIA

Pompey's attack

Dium

Scythopolis
Pella

J U D E A

Coreae

Jericho
Jerusalem

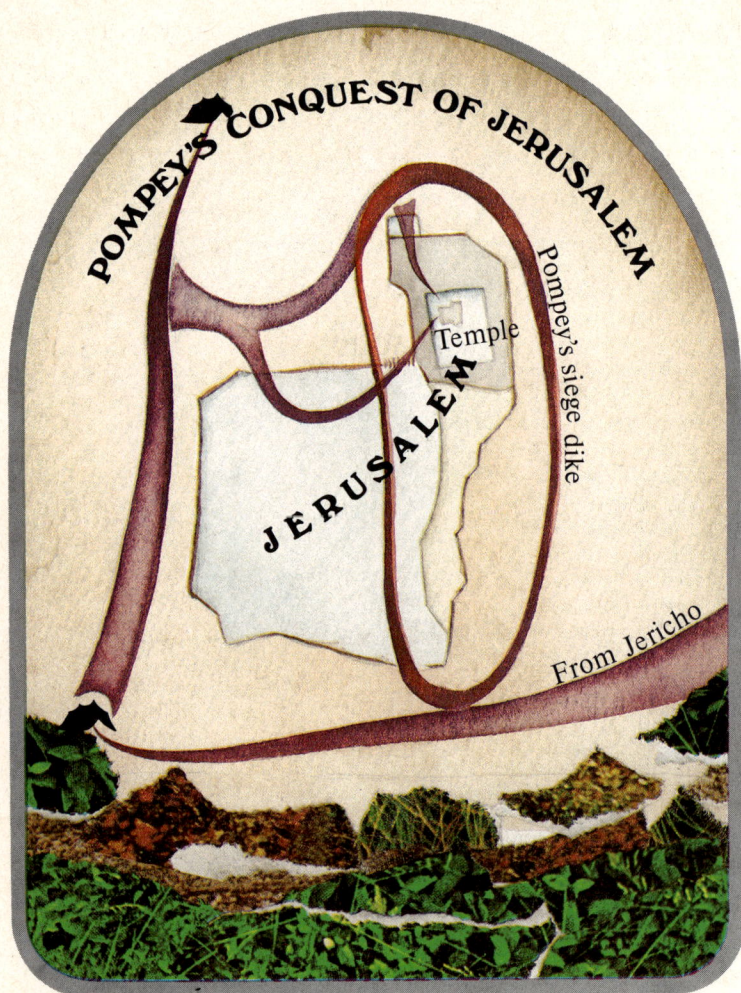

POMPEY'S CONQUEST OF JERUSALEM

Temple

JERUSALEM

Pompey's siege dike

From Jericho

# THE RULE OF ROME

*(Josephus, Antiquities 14-17;*
*Jewish War 1-2)*

63 BCE-CE 6

Unrest continued in the area, and war and conflict between the large empires of the region resulted in the Jews of that period trying to continue a life of their own whilst ignoring the political changes around them. The Sanhedrin, which consisted of 71 learned and respected men, continued to be the supreme authority on all legal and religious matters concerning the Jewish population and they had the power to administer punishment even to the penalty of death. However, this right was taken from them in the year 30 CE when the Romans ordered that only the Roman governor could pass sentence of death.

Pompey's success in Judea was to be followed a few years later by serious revolts and in 52 BCE the Temple was occupied and robbed. It was not until Julius Caesar became first consul of Rome that the Jews felt that they had a friend and helper. His assassination in 44 BCE was a great blow to the Jews in the area of Judea. It was soon after this event that the leaders of the Parthian Empire decided to invade Syria and Judea banishing the Romans for, what was to be, a short period. Very soon the Romans recovered the land which they had lost and it was Mark Antony and his legions who captured Jerusalem in 36 BCE — exactly the same day as Pompey had taken the city 26 years earlier. An officer named Herod, who was previously collector-in-chief for taxes was proclaimed by the Romans as King of Judea.

Herod was not a Jew by birth but converted, together with other Edomites, to Judaism in the time of the Hasmonean king Yochanan Hyrcanus and married Mariamne of the Hasmonean dynasty. Hyrcanus also waged a successful war against the Samaritans and destroyed their temple on Mount Gerizim. Herod tried to show his loyalty to Judaism by rebuilding the Temple which had originally been built in the time of Ezra. Herod employed more than 11,000 people for nine years in order to erect a magnificent extended Temple. However, he could not win over the hearts of the Jewish people because his other actions made them still regard him as an agent for the power of Rome.

It was during this period in Jewish history that the cultural aspect of Judaism began to grow which was to influence Jews throughout the world for

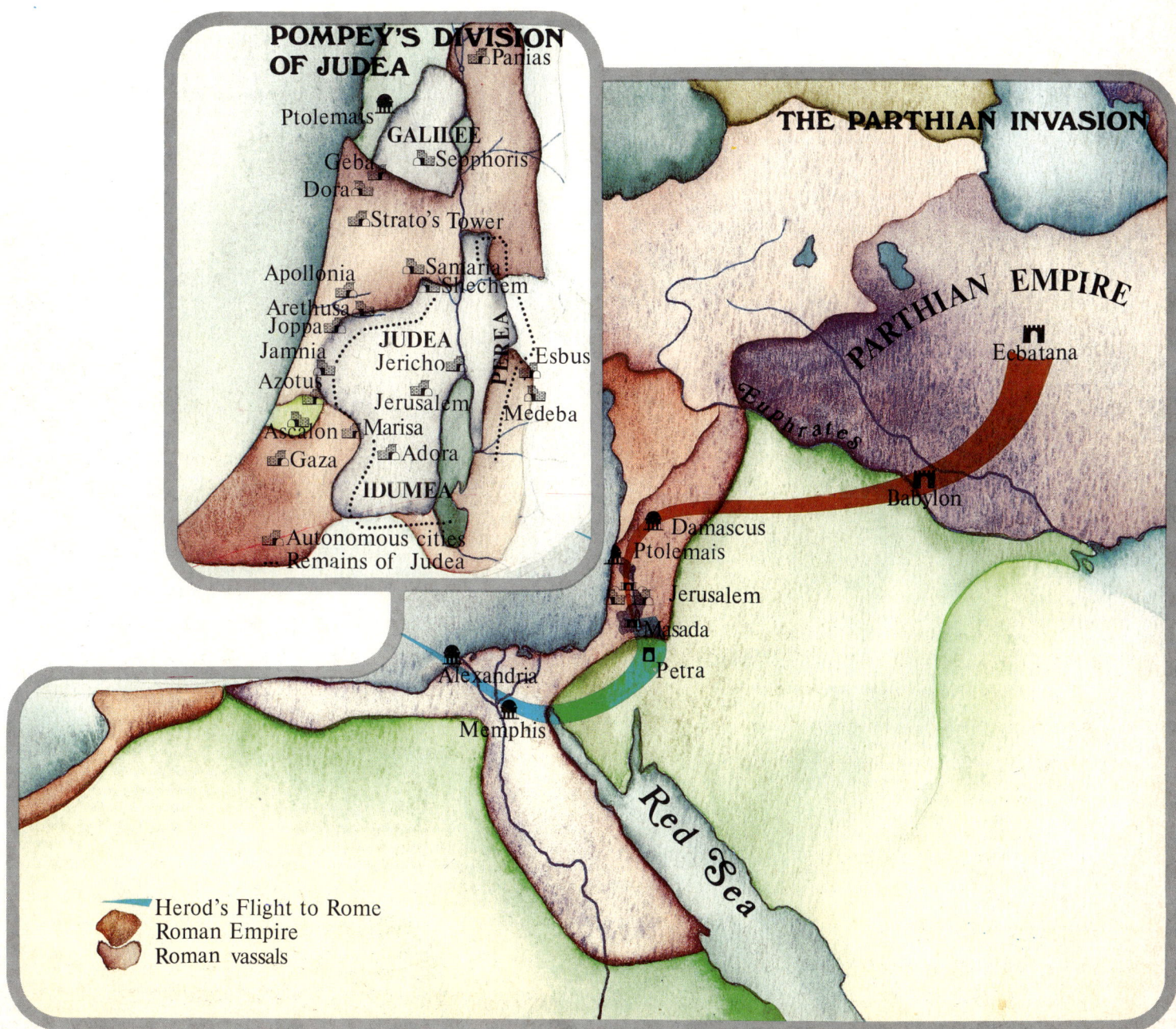

**POMPEY'S DIVISION OF JUDEA**

Panias
Ptolemais
GALILEE
Geba · Sepphoris
Dora
Strato's Tower
Apollonia · Samaria
Shechem
Arethusa
Joppa
Jamnia
JUDEA
PEREA
Jericho · Esbus
Azotus
Jerusalem
Ascalon · Marisa · Medeba
Gaza · Adora
IDUMEA

Autonomous cities
Remains of Judea

**THE PARTHIAN INVASION**

PARTHIAN EMPIRE
Ecbatana
Euphrates
Babylon
Damascus
Ptolemais
Jerusalem
Masada
Petra
Alexandria
Memphis

Red Sea

Herod's Flight to Rome
Roman Empire
Roman vassals

## HEROD'S KINGDOM

GAULANITIS TRACHONITIS
GALILEE
BATANEA
AURANITIS
Caesarea
Sebaste
SAMARIA
PEREA
JUDEA
Herodium
Macherus
Masada
Herod's additions

## SECOND TEMPLE PERIOD

**520 BCE**
Building of Second Temple.
Partial return to Judah.
Reconstruction under Ezra
and Nehemiah.

**333 BCE**
Alexander the Great of
Greece conquers the Middle
East.
Beginning of Hellenistic
influence.

**323-200 BCE**
Domination by Ptolemies.

**200 BCE**
Conquest by Seleucids.

**167 BCE**
Uprising under Judas
Maccabeus.

**141 BCE**
Judea independent.
Hasmonean dynasty.

## HEROD'S JERUSALEM

Antonia Fortress
Temple
Phasael Hippicus
Mariamne
Herod's Palace
UPPER CITY
LOWER CITY
Herod's Construction

THE DEAD SEA SECT (THE ESSENES)

Beth-shean

SAMARIA

Mt. Gerizim

R. Jordan

JUDEA

PEREA

Nebo

Mesad Hasidim
(Qumran)

Dead Sea

IDUMEA

Masada

········ Dwelling area of the Essenes
Alleged Essene caches

HEROD'S KINGDOM DIVIDED

GALILEE H

GAULANITIS TRACHONITIS
BATANEA P
AURANITIS

Mediterranean Sea

SAMARIA

A

JUDEA

PEREA H

IDUMEA

A Archelaus
H Herod Antipas
P Philip

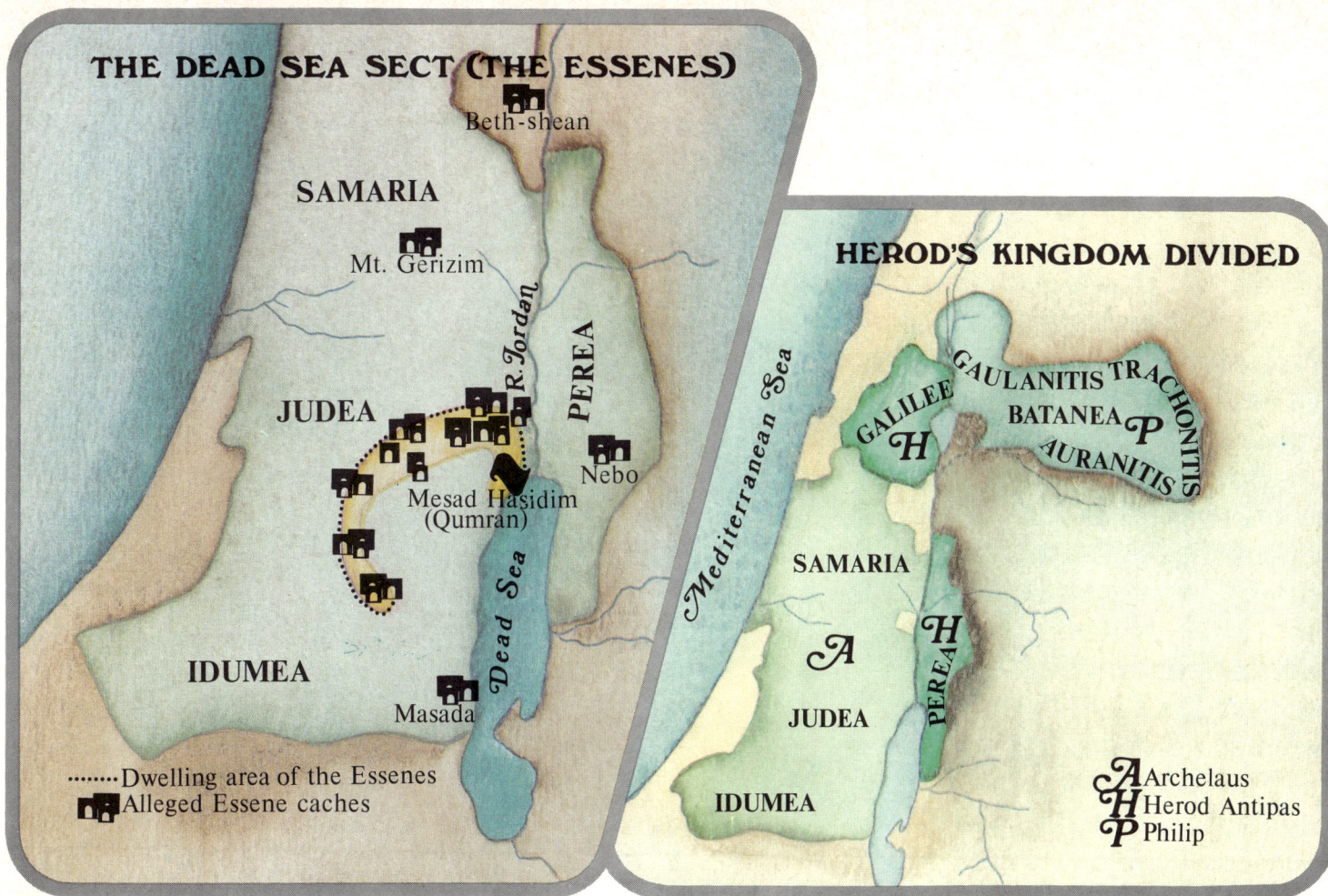

future generations. This all happened at the same time in Judea, Babylonia and in the Greek-speaking part of the world with Alexandria in Egypt as its centre. It was then that the Talmud — the encyclopaedic work explaining the Torah and formulating its laws — was produced both in Judea and in Babylonia. Great teachers such as Hillel and Shammai, Shemaiah and Avtalion, led the discussions and made decisions as well as setting ethical and moral standards which became proverbial for all time. It took over 500 years to complete. At the same time, through the loss of the Hebrew language by the Hellenistic Jews, the sacred writings were translated into Greek for the Greek-speaking Jews. Although it was not realised at the time, this translation which was eventually translated into every known language, was to have an influence on the religious and secular thought of all mankind.

Herod the Great, as he was known, did not enjoy his reign of 33 years, which included a series of murders and outrages against prominent Jewish leaders as well as against his own family. When Herod died in the year 43 CE the whole of his kingdom was divided by the Romans, according to Herod's will between his sons, Archelaus, Antipas and Philip. But very soon the Roman Emperor Augustus saw that trouble was on the way through Archelaus's inability to rule Judea, so he appointed his own governors for the region. These governors were only interested in enforcing exorbitant taxation on the people of Judea.

Eventually this high taxation caused outbursts of rebellion among the Jews of the area.

## THE REVOLTS OF THE JEWS AGAINST ROME

*(Josephus, Jewish War 2-7)*
CE 55-74; 132-135

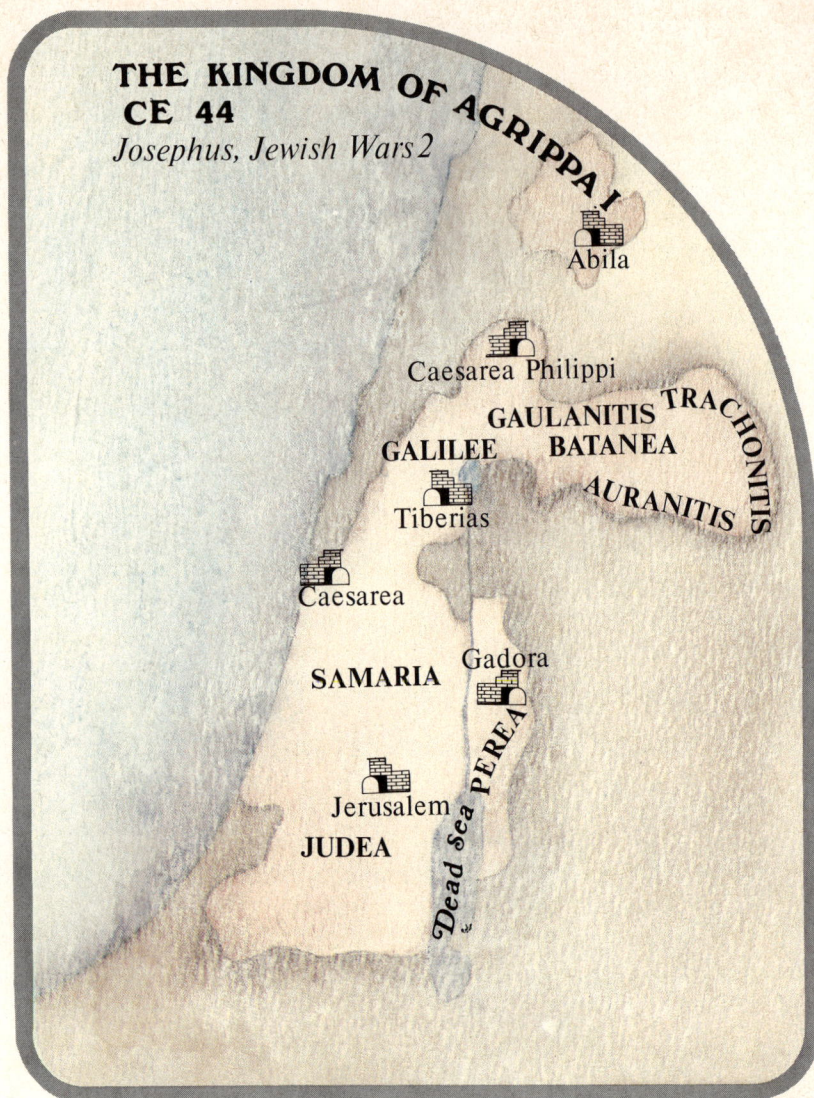

THE KINGDOM OF AGRIPPA I
CE 44
*Josephus, Jewish Wars 2*

Abila

Caesarea Philippi

GAULANITIS
GALILEE    BATANEA    TRACHONTIS
Tiberias              AURANITIS

Caesarea

SAMARIA    Gadora
                    PEREA

Jerusalem    Dead Sea
JUDEA

**B**esides paying high taxes to the Romans, tithes and Temple dues had to be given by the Jews as part of their religious duties. A number of governors were sent by Rome to Judea, some better than others, but none of them could really prevent the feeling of rebellion among the Jews who could tolerate the situation no longer. Rebellion became open and organised revolt against the Romans. In the year 66 BCE the Jews overpowered the Roman garrison in Jerusalem and this caused the Roman emperor to send the famous general Vespasian to quell the revolt. With the assistance of the Syrians it took the Romans four long years to complete the conquest. Jerusalem and its Temple had become the stronghold and strongest point of defence for the Jews, but finally on the ninth day of the Hebrew month of Av, the Temple was destroyed, except for part of the Western Wall which stands to this day.

When Jerusalem fell, the war was practically at an end; however, three fortresses held out even after the destruction of the capital. One of these, called Masada, near the Dead Sea, and built by Herod a century earlier, was in a sense never taken by the Romans, because in the end, rather than surrender and be captured by the Romans, the 960 Jews decided to commit suicide. The Romans entered the silent city only to find corpses and burnt-down dwellings. Today this flat-topped fortress, situated in the desolation of the Judean Desert and high above the blue waters of the Dead Sea, is a source of inspiration and courage, symbolised by the slogan found on the top of the fortress — "Masada shall not fall again".

But the catastrophe of the fall of Jerusalem did not mark the end of the Jewish religion or the Jewish people. The centre of religious activity became Yavneh, headed by Rabbi Yochanan Ben Zakkai. From time to time spasmodic revolts flared up culminating in rebellion lead by the warrior Bar Kochba which resulted in the fall of Beitar, the last Jewish stronghold, and also the death of Bar Kochba in the year 135. The Jews had fought the Romans for something which was precious to them since the Exodus from Egypt — freedom.

Victory was not theirs, but they continued as a people even without a land or a true language of their own, except for the Hebrew language used at service and for study. Their faith, through their Torah, lasted for 40 centuries, often in terrible anguish and suffering, including the Holocaust, until 1948, when the re-birth of a Jewish homeland came into being with the establishment of the State of Israel through the majority vote in its favour at the United Nations in November 1947.

THE JEWISH REVOLT AGAINST ROME CE 66
*Josephus, Jewish Wars 2*

SYRIA
Roman Legion
Captured by rebels
DECAPOLIS
Judea under Roman procurators
JUDEA
Main area of Revolt
Lydda
Beth-Horon
Cyprus
Jerusalem
Dead Sea
Macherus
Masada

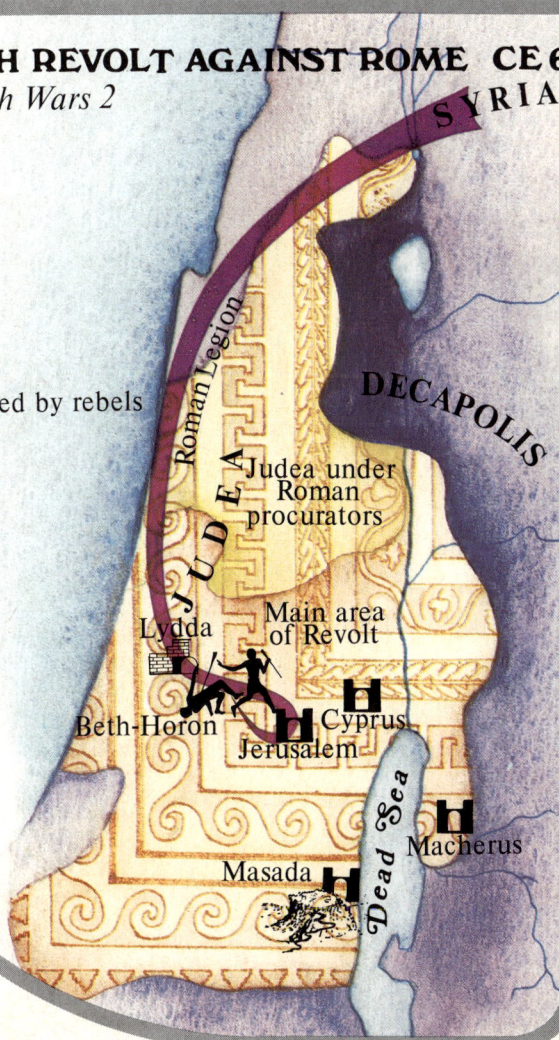

JEWISH MILITARY REGIONS AFTER CE 66
GALILEE
Sepphoris
Joppa
Gadora
Gophna
JUDEA
Jericho
Jerusalem
Betogabris

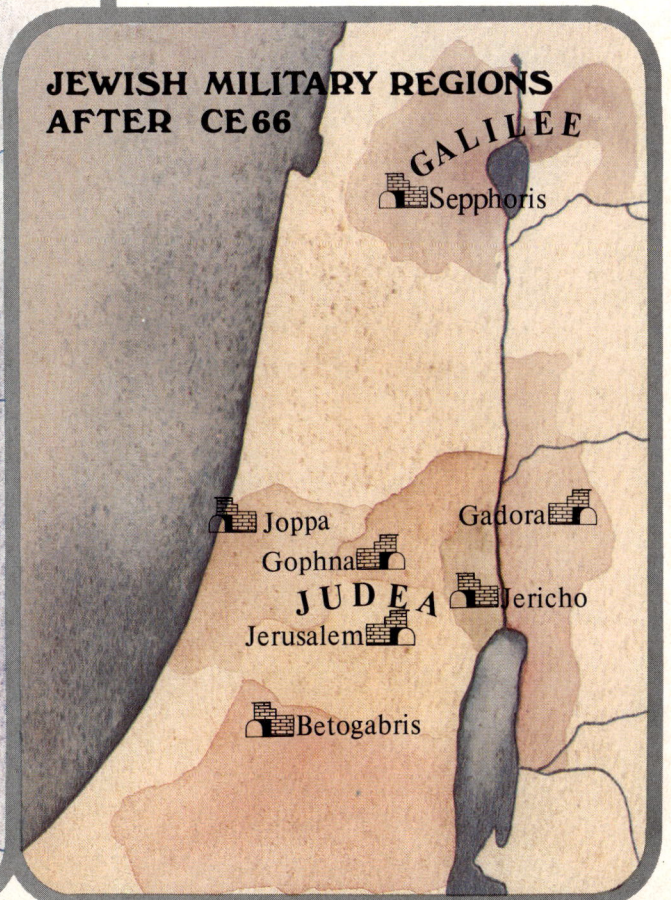

# THE ROMAN ATTACK ON JERUSALEM CE 70

*Josephus, Jewish Wars 5*

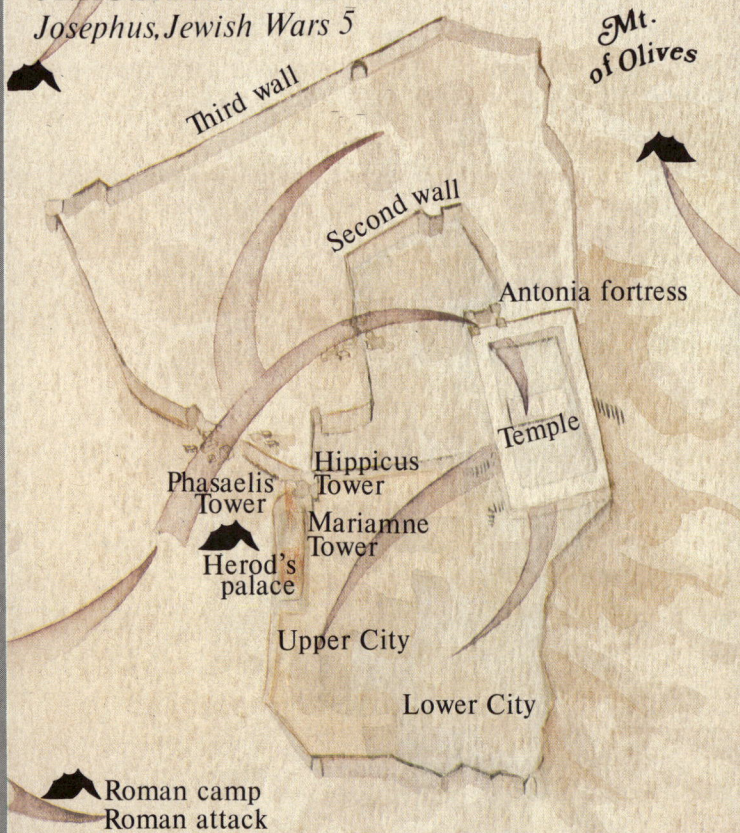

Mt. of Olives

Third wall

Second wall

Antonia fortress

Temple

Phasaelis Tower

Hippicus Tower

Mariamne Tower

Herod's palace

Upper City

Lower City

🔺 Roman camp
Roman attack

# THE CONQUEST OF THE LAST REBEL STRONGHOLDS

*Josephus, Jewish Wars 4*

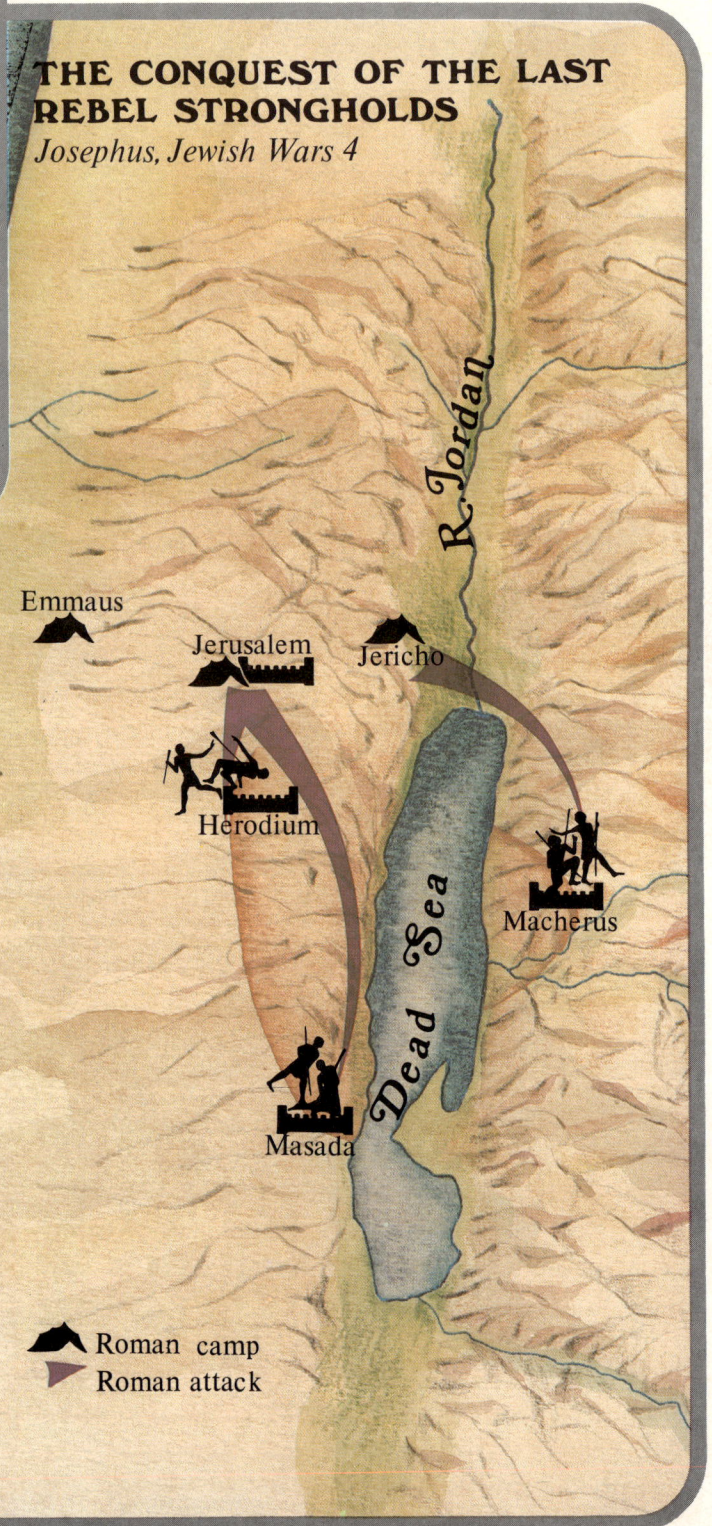

Emmaus

Jerusalem

Jericho

R. Jordan

Herodium

Macherus

Dead Sea

Masada

🔺 Roman camp
Roman attack

# VESPASIAN CONQUERS THE GALILEE AND JUDEA

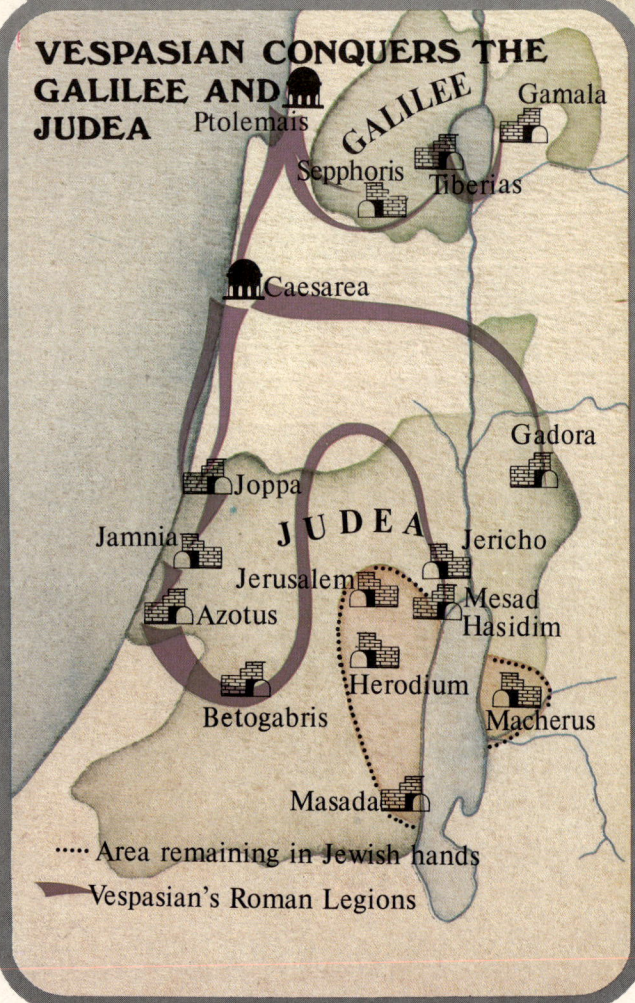

Ptolemais

GALILEE

Gamala

Sepphoris

Tiberias

Caesarea

Gadora

Joppa

JUDEA

Jericho

Jamnia

Jerusalem

Mesad Hasidim

Azotus

Herodium

Macherus

Betogabris

Masada

····· Area remaining in Jewish hands

Vespasian's Roman Legions

The prayers recited three times a day, at meal times and on both happy and sad occasions, had been answered. The many who had toiled, cleared the swamps and made the desert bloom did not do so in vain. The spiritual, cultural, technical and scientific achievements of the modern state serve as a reminder of the tremendous strides that can be made benefiting Jew and non-Jew, and indeed all humanity, if there is peace in the area. As the prophet Isaiah declared: "For out of Zion shall go forth the Law, and the word of the Lord from Jerusalem."

**JUDEA BETWEEN THE REVOLTS   CE 73-131**

Roman colony
Main concentration of Jewish communities
Seat of Sanhedrin

Tyre

Capernaum
Bethsaida-Julias

Ptolemais
Rimmon
Cochaba

Mediterranean Sea

Caesarea
Pella

Samaria-Sebaste

Neapolis

Joppa
Lydda
PROVINCE OF JUDEA

Jamnia

Azotus
Jerusalem

Dead Sea

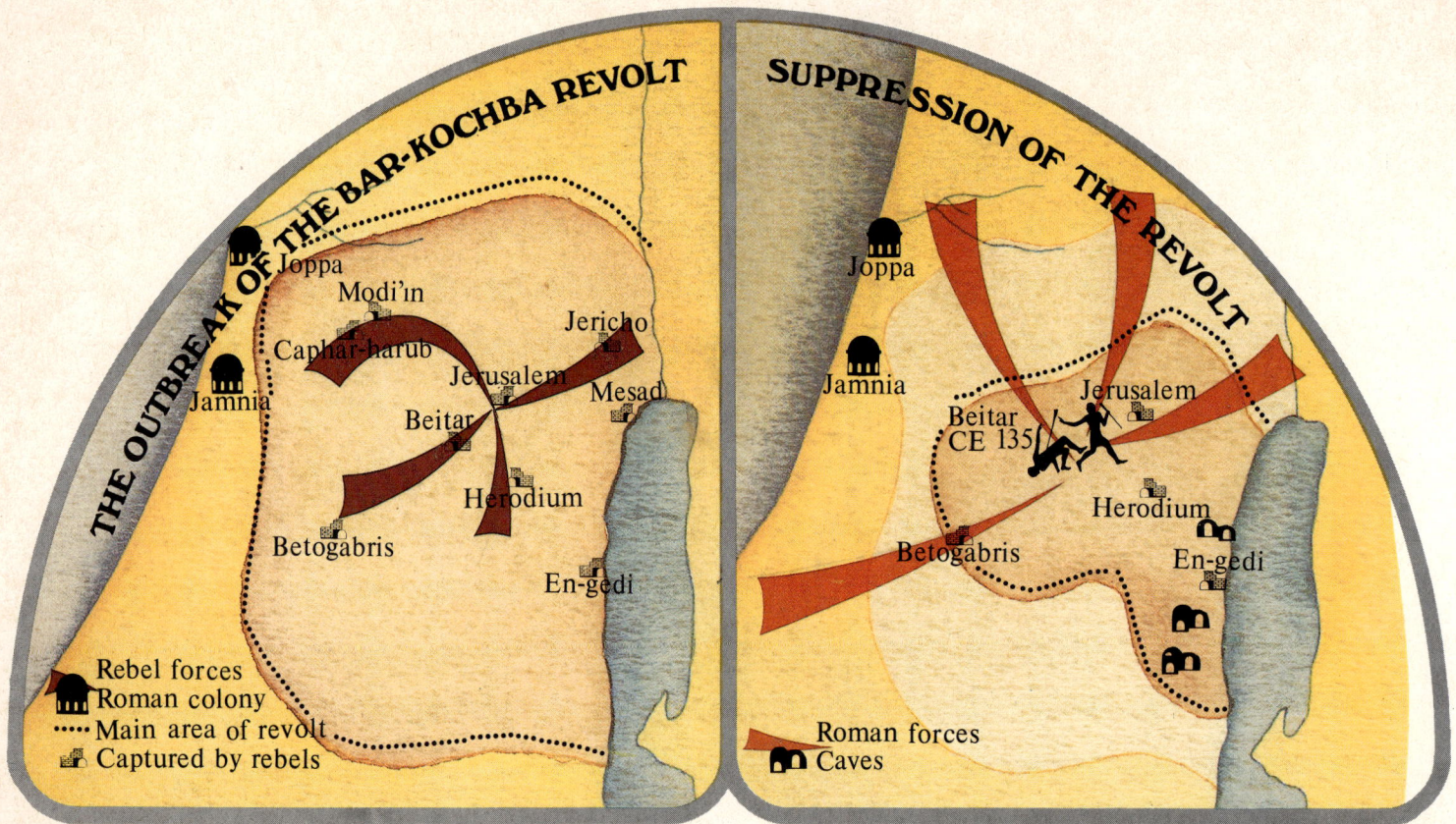

Joppa
Modi'in
Caphar-harub
Jamnia
Jericho
Jerusalem
Mesad
Beitar
Herodium
Betogabris
En-gedi

◣ Rebel forces
🏛 Roman colony
⋯ Main area of revolt
🏚 Captured by rebels

Joppa
Jamnia
Jerusalem
Beitar CE 135
Herodium
Betogabris
En-gedi

◣ Roman forces
🏚 Caves

## ROMAN PERIOD

### 63 BCE
Conquest by Pompey.
Roman rule: Jewish settlement restricted to
Galilee and Judea.

### 37 BCE-4 CE
Herod the Great.

### 66 CE
Revolt against Romans.
Troops under Vespasian despatched by
Emperor Nero.

### 70 CE
Fall of Jerusalem and destruction of Temple by
Titus.

### 73 CE
Fall of Masada.
Religous centre at Yavneh.

### 117 CE
Emperor Hadrian — persecutions.

### 132-135 CE
Revolt under Bar Kochba followed by period of
peace.

Tyre

Dan

Hazor

Tiberias

Nazareth

En-dor

Megiddo

Caesarea

Samaria

Abel-meholah

Shechem

Mahanaim

Shiloh

Penuel

*The Great Sea*

Joppa

Gezer

Mizpah

Jericho

Gilgal

Jerusalem

Ramah

Azotus

Bethlehem

Qumran

Herodium

Ascalon

Hebron

En-Gedi

Gaza

Eshtemoa

Masada

Ziklag

Beer-sheba

Sodom

Elusa

Migdol

Kadesh-barnea

Timna

Ezion-geber

# INDEX TO MAPS

## A

עַבְדוֹן — Abdon 24
אָבֵל בֵּית מַעֲכָה — Abel-beth-maacah 39, 42
אָבֵל מְחוֹלָה — Abel-meholah 42, 75
אָבֵל שִׁטִּים — Abel-shittim 20
אֲבִילָה — Abila 65, 70
עַכּוֹ — Acco 22
אַכְשָׁף — Achshaph 21
אַכְזִיב — Achzib 22
עֲקְרַבָּה — Acrabeta 62
חָדִיד — Adida 65
אֲדוֹרַיִם — Adora 67
עֲדֻלָּם — Adullam 32, 44, 52, 55
הַיָּם הָאֵיגֵאִי — Aegean Sea 22
אַחְלָב — Ahlab 22
אָחָז — Ahaz 50
הָעַי — Ai 14, 21
אַיָּלוֹן — Aijalon 22, 34, 44
אַחְ׳תָאתֹן — Akhetaton 15
אַכַּד — Akkad 11
אֲלֶכְסַנְדְּרִיָה — Alexandria 58, 67
אֲלֶכְסַנְדְּרִיוֹן — Alexandrium 65
עֲמָלֵקִים — Amalekites 30, 31, 33
חַמְתָן — Ammathus 65
עַמּוֹן — Ammon 22, 26, 34, 36, 38, 39, 42, 44, 49, 50
אַנְתֵדוֹן — Anthedon 65
אַנְטִיוֹכְיָה — Antioch 58
אַנְטִיוֹכְיָה — Antiochia 61, 65
אַנְטִיוֹכְיָה (הִיפּוֹס) — Antiochia (Hippus) 61
אַנְטִיוֹכְיָה יְרוּשָׁלַיִם — Antiochia Jerusalem 61
אֲפֵק — Aphek 22, 33, 46, 52, 55
אֲפּוֹלוֹנְיָה — Apollonia 61, 65, 67
הָעֲרָבָה — Arabah 18, 36
עֲרָב — Arabia 41, 47, 58
מִדְבָּר — Arabian Desert 10, 12
עֲרָד — Arad 40
אֲרַם דַּמֶּשֶׂק — Aram-Damascus 37, 39, 42, 44, 45, 46, 47, 50
אֲרַם צוֹבָה — Aram-zobah 36, 37
אֲרֵתוּסָה — Arethusa 67
אַרְגֹּב — Argob 42
עֲרוֹעֵר — Aroer 42, 49
אַרְוָד — Arvad 47
אָסָה — Asa 45
אַשְׁקְלוֹן (אַשְׁקְלוֹן) — Ascalon 67, 75 (see Ashkelon)
עָשָׁן — Ashan 40
אַשְׁדּוֹד — Ashdod 23, 27, 28
אַשְׁקְלוֹן — Ashkelon 23, 27

אָשֵׁר — Asher 22, 31, 34, 39
אַסְיָה — Asia Minor 23
אַסְוָן — Aswan 15
עַשְׁתָּרוֹת — Ashtaroth 42, 49
אַשּׁוּר — Assyria 13, 47, 48, 51, 54
אַשּׁוּר (מַמְלָכָה) — Assyrian Empire 53
חַוְרָן — Auranitis 68, 69, 70
עֵמֶק אַיָּלוֹן — Ayalon, Valley of 21
עֲזֵקָה — Azekah 21, 31, 34, 44, 55
אַזוֹטוֹס (אַשְׁדּוֹד) — Azotus 61, 62, 67, 72, 73, 75
אַזוֹטוֹס פַּרַלִיוֹס — Azotus Paralius 61

## B

בַּעֲלַת בְּאֵר — Baalath-beer 40
בַּעַל חָצוֹר — Baal-hazor 38
בַּעַל מְעֹן — Baal-meon 62
בַּעַל פְּרָצִים — Baal-perazim 34
בַּעַל צָפוֹן — Baal-zephon 17
בַּעְשָׁה — Baasha 45
בָּבֶל — Babylon 11, 12, 51, 53, 54, 55, 56, 58, 67
בָּבֶל (מַמְלָכה) — Babylonian Empire 54, 56
בַּחוּרִים — Bahurim 38
בָּרָק — Barak 24
הַבָּשָׁן — Bashan 18, 42
בַּתָנֵיָה — Batanea 68, 69, 70
בְּאֵר לַחַי רֹאִי — Beer-lahai-roi 14
בְּאֵרוֹת — Beeroth 21
בְּאֵר שֶׁבַע — Beer-sheba 14, 37, 40, 55, 75
בֵּיתָר — Beitar 74
בִּנְיָמִין — Benjamin 22, 26, 28, 29, 30, 31, 34, 39
בֵּית עֲבָרָה — Bethabara 75
בֵּית עֲנָת — Beth-anath 22
בֵּית חוֹרוֹן — Beth-horon 21, 40, 71
בֵּית חוֹרוֹן תַּחְתּוֹן — Beth-horon, Lower 34
בֵּית חוֹרוֹן עֶלְיוֹן — Beth-horon, Upper 34, 62
בֵּית בַּעַל מְעוֹן — Beth-baal-meon 42
בֵּית אֵל — Bethel 14, 21, 29, 44, 45
בֵּית לֶחֶם — Bethlehem 14, 34, 42, 44, 75
בֵּית צַיְדָא — Bethsaida 73, 75
בֵּית שְׁאָן — Beth-shean 22, 33, 34, 42, 69
בֵּית שֶׁמֶשׁ — Beth-shemesh 22, 28, 34, 40, 42
בֵּית צוּר — Beth-zur 65
בֵּית גּוּבְרִין — Betogabris 71, 72, 74
נַחַל מִצְרַיִם — Brook of Egypt 18, 27
בוּקוֹלוֹן פוֹלִיס — Bucolon Polis 61
גְּבָל — Byblos 47

## C

קֵיסָרִי — Caesarea 68, 70, 72, 73, 75
קֵיסַרְיוֹן — Caesarea Philippi 70
קָהִיר — Cairo 13, 15

כֶּלַח Calah 51
קָנָה Cana 75
כְּנַעַן Canaan 11, 12, 15, 16, 17, 18, 19, 22, 23
כְּנַעֲנִים Canaanites 14
כְּפַר נַחוּם Capernaum 73, 75
כְּפַר חָרוּב Caphar-harub 74
כַּפְתּוֹר Caphtor 23
קַפָּדוֹקְיָה Cappadocia 13
כַּרְכְּמִישׁ Carchemish 53
הַר הַכַּרְמֶל Carmel, Mt. 25
כְּפִירָה Chephirah 21
נְהַר כְּבָר Chebar 55
כִּנֶּרֶת Chinnereth 45
יָם כִּנֶּרֶת Chinnereth, Sea of 21, 25, 26, 31, 42
כּוֹרָזִין Chorazin 75
קִילִיקְיָה Cilicia 41
כּוֹכָבָה Cochaba 73
קוֹרָאִי Coreae 65
עִיר הַתַּנִּינִים Crocodilon Polis 61
כּוּתָה Cuthah 51
קַפְרִיסִין Cyprus 71

# D

דַּמֶּשֶׂק Damascus 36, 37, 44, 45, 46, 47, 48, 49, 50, 51, 65, 67
דָּן Dan 19, 22, 23, 42, 44, 45, 75
דָּוִד David 31, 33, 34
יָם הַמֶּלַח Dead Sea 14, 20, 21, 22, 26, 27, 28, 29, 31, 32, 33, 35, 38, 42, 52, 61, 65, 69, 70, 71, 72, 73
דְּבִר Debir 21
דְּבוֹרָה Deborah 24
דֶּקַפּוֹלִיס Decapolis 71
דִּיּוֹן Dium 65
דּוֹר Dor (Dora) 22, 42, 65, 67
דֹּתָן Dothan 15

# E

אֶקְבַּטָנָה Ecbatana 56, 67
אֱדוֹם Edom 18, 22, 36, 37, 44, 45, 50
עֶגְלוֹן Eglon 21
מִצְרַיִם Egypt 11, 12, 13, 15, 16, 17, 23, 37, 41, 53, 54, 58
אֵהוּד Ehud 24, 26
עֶקְרוֹן Ekron 23, 27, 28
אֵילַת Elath 18, 36, 40, 49, 50
עֵילָם Elam (Persia) 13, 54
אֱלִישָׁה Elishah 23
אֵילוֹן Elon 24
חֲלוּצָה Elusa 75

אֶמָּאוּס Emmaus 62, 72
עֵין דּוֹר En-dor 26, 75
עֵין גֶּדִי En-gedi 32, 74, 75
עֵין גִּיחוֹן En-gihon 43
עֵין חֲרֹד En-harod 26
עֵין רֹגֵל En-rogel 39
אֶפְרַיִם Ephraim 22, 26, 28, 29, 30, 31, 34, 39
יַעַר אֶפְרַיִם Ephraim, Forest of 38
הַר אֶפְרַיִם Ephraim, Mt. 42
אֶרֶךְ Erech 11
חֶשְׁבּוֹן Esbus 67
אֶשְׁבַּעַל Eshbaal 34
אֶשְׁתְּמוֹעַ Eshtemoa 75
כּוּשׁ Ethiopia 41
נְהַר פְּרָת Euphrates, R. 10, 11, 13, 16, 47, 50, 51, 54, 55, 67
עֶצְיוֹן גֶּבֶר Ezion-geber 40, 45, 75

# G

גָּד Gad 22, 42, 51
גֶּדֶר Gadara 65, 74
גְּדוֹר Gadora 70, 71, 72
הַגָּלִיל Galilee 19, 67, 68, 69, 70, 72
גַּמְלָה Gamala 65, 72
גַּת Gath 23, 27, 28, 31, 32, 34, 37, 39, 42, 52
גַּת הַחֵפֶר Gath-hepher 42
גַּת רִמּוֹן Gath-rimmon 42
גּוּגַמְלָה Gaugamela 58
גּוֹלָנִיטִיס Gaulanitis 68, 69, 70
עַזָּה Gaza 21, 23, 27, 45, 58, 65, 67, 75
גָּזֶר Gazara 65
גֶּבַע Geba 30, 34, 45, 67
גְּרָר Gerar 14
גֶּרָסָה Gerasa 65
הַר גְּרִזִים Gerizim, Mt. 69
גֶּזֶר Gezer 22, 27, 28, 34, 40, 45, 75
גְּשׁוּר Geshur 36, 37, 39, 42, 44
גִּבְעָה Gibeah 29, 30, 31, 32, 34
גִּבְעוֹן Gibeon 21, 29, 34, 39, 42
גִּדְעוֹן Gideon 24, 26
הַר הַגִּלְבֹּעַ Gilboa, Mt. 33
גִּלְעָד Gilead 18, 26, 30, 31, 34, 51, 62
גִּלְגָּל Gilgal 20, 21, 29, 30, 75
גִּתַּיִם Gittaim 55
גּוֹפְנָה Gophna 62, 71
הָרֵי גוֹפְנָה Gophna Hills 62
גֹּשֶׁן Goshen 15, 17
גּוֹזָן Gozan 51
הַיָּם הַגָּדוֹל Great Sea 12, 14, 16, 18, 22, 23, 27, 31, 32, 33, 34, 37, 40, 42, 45, 46, 47, 48, 49, 50, 53, 54, 55, 75

# H

| חָבוֹר | Habor 51 |
| חָם | Ham 10 |
| חֲמָת | Hamath 36, 37, 46, 47, 48, 51 |
| חָרָן | Haran 12, 13, 53 |
| חַתּוּשָׁשׁ | Hattusa 16 |
| חֲצַר אַדָּר | Hazar-addar 40 |
| חֲצֵרוֹת | Hazeroth 17 |
| חָצוֹר | Hazor 21, 25, 40, 42, 45, 48, 49, 75 |
| חֶבְרוֹן | Hebron 14, 15, 21, 33, 35, 38, 42, 44, 52, 62, 75 |
| חֵילָם | Helam 36 |
| חֵפֶר | Hepher 42 |
| הַר חֶרְמוֹן | Hermon, Mt. 19 |
| הֵרוֹדְיוֹן | Herodium 68, 72, 74, 75 |
| חֶשְׁבּוֹן | Heshbon 42 |
| הִיפּוֹס | Hippus 65, 75 |
| מַמְלֶכֶת הַחִתִּים | Hittite Empire 16 |
| הוֹרְקַנְיָה | Hyrcania 65 |

# I

| יִבְלְעָם | Ibleam 22 |
| אִבְצָן | Ibzan 24 |
| אֲדוֹמְיָה | Idumea 62, 67, 69 |
| הוֹדוּ | India 41, 58 |
| הָאוֹקְיָנוֹס הַהוֹדִי | Indian Ocean 58 |
| אִינְדוֹס | Indus, River 58 |
| יִשְׂרָאֵל | Israel 34, 35, 37, 38, 39, 44, 45, 46, 47, 48, 49, 50, 51 |
| יִשָּׂשכָר | Issachar 22, 25, 26, 39, 42 |
| אִיסוֹס | Issus 58 |
| אִיטַבִּירְיוֹן | Itabyrium 61 |

# J

| יַבֹּק, נַחַל | Jabbok R. 18, 38 |
| יָבֵשׁ גִּלְעָד | Jabesh-gilead 30, 33, 42 |
| יַהְצָה | Jahzah 18 |
| יָאִיר | Jair 24 |
| יַמְנְיָה | Jamnia 61, 62, 67, 72, 73, 74 |
| יַמְנְיָה פַּרְלִיוֹס | Jamnia, port of 61 |
| יֶפֶת | Japheth 10 |
| יַרְמוּת | Jarmuth 21 |
| יַעְזֵר | Jazer 62 |
| יְבוּס | Jebus 22, 24, 28, 29, 30, 31, 32, 33, 34, 35 |
| יִפְתָּח | Jephthah 24, 26 |
| יְרִיחוֹ | Jericho 19, 26, 55, 65, 67, 71, 72, 74, 75 |
| יָרָבְעָם | Jeroboam 49 |
| יְרוּשָׁלַיִם | Jerusalem 14, 21, 34, 35, 36, 37, 38, 39, 40, 42, 44, 45, 46, 48, 49, 50, 52, 55, 56, 58, 62, 65, 66, 67, 70, 71, 72, 73, 74, 75 |
| יִזְרְעֶאל | Jezreel 31, 33 |
| עֵמֶק יִזְרְעֶאל | Jezreel, Plain of 21, 25 |
| יְהוֹנָתָן | Jonathan 30 |
| יָפוֹ | Joppa 28, 52, 62, 67, 71, 72, 73, 74, 75 |
| הַיַּרְדֵּן | Jordan, R. 12, 13, 14, 15, 19, 20, 25, 26, 29, 31, 35, 38, 40, 49, 55, 62, 69, 72 |
| יָטְבָתָה | Jotbathah 40 |
| יְהוּדָה | Judah 22, 27, 28, 30, 31, 32, 34, 35, 37, 39, 42, 44, 45, 46, 47, 48, 49, 50, 51, 52, 53, 55 |
| יְהוּדָה הַמַּקַבִּי | Judas 62 |
| יְהוּדָה | Judea 60, 62, 65, 67, 68, 69, 70, 71, 72 |
| יוּדֵיאָה | Judea, Province of 85 |

# K

| קָדֵשׁ | Kadesh 16 |
| קָדֵשׁ בַּרְנֵעַ | Kadesh-barnea 17, 18, 75 |
| קָנָה | Kanah 42 |
| קַנְדְהַר | Kandahar 58 |
| קֶדֶשׁ נַפְתָּלִי | Kedesh-naphtali 25 |
| קְעִילָה | Keilah 32 |
| נַחַל קִדְרוֹן | Kidron Valley 57 |
| דֶּרֶךְ הַמֶּלֶךְ | King's Highway 11 |
| קִרְיַת אַרְבַּע (חֶבְרוֹן) | Kiriath-arba (Hebron) 55 |
| קִרְיַת יְעָרִים | Kiriath-jearim 21, 35 |
| קִיר מוֹאָב | Kir-moab 36 |
| נַחַל קִישׁוֹן | Kishon, R. 25 |

# L

| לָכִישׁ | Lachish 21, 44, 52, 55 |
| לְבָנוֹן | Lebanon 40, 58 |
| לְבוֹא חֲמָת | Lebo-hamath 18, 49 |
| לִבְנָה | Libnah 21, 52 |
| לֹד | Lod 28, 55 |
| הַיָּם הַתַּחְתּוֹן | Lower Sea 54 |
| לֹד | Lydda (Lod) 71, 73 |

# M

| מַעֲכָה | Maacah 37 |
| מוֹקְדוֹן | Macedonia 58 |
| מַכְוֵר | Macherus 65, 68, 71, 72 |
| מָדוֹן | Madon (Merom) 21 |
| מַחֲנַיִם | Mahanaim 14, 34, 38, 39, 42, 75 |
| מַמְפְּסִיס | Mampsis 75 |
| מַמְרֵא | Mamre 14 |
| מָנַחַת | Manahath 34 |
| מְנַשֶּׁה | Manasseh 22, 26, 28, 39, 51 |

מָעוֹן Maon 32

מַרְקַנְדָּה Maracanda 58

מָרִיסָה Marisa 61, 62, 67

מְצָדָה Masada 65, 67, 68, 69, 71, 72, 75

מֵידְבָּא Medeba 36, 67

מָדַי Media 51, 53

מַמְלֶכֶת מָדַי Median Empire 54, 56

הַיָּם הַתִּיכוֹן Mediterranean Sea 10, 11, 58, 61, 69, 73

מְגִדּוֹ Megiddo 25, 37, 40, 45, 51, 53, 55, 75

מֶמְפִיס Memphis 13, 15, 58, 67

מְצַד חֲסִידִים (קוּמְרָאן) Mesad Hasidim (Qumran) 69, 72, 74

מֶשְׁהֶד Meshed 58

מֶסוֹפוֹטַמְיָה Mesopotamia 11, 12

מִכְמָשׁ Michmash 30

מִדְיָנִים Midianites 26

מִגְדּוֹל Migdol 17, 75

מִשְׂרְפוֹת מַיִם Misrephot-maim 21

מִיתַנִּי (מַמְלָכָה) Mitanni Empire 16

מִצְפָּה Mizpah 29, 30, 45, 55, 75

מוֹאָב Moab 18, 22, 26, 34, 36, 37, 44, 45, 46, 50

מוֹאָבִי Moabites 30, 31

עַרְבוֹת מוֹאָב Moab, Plains of 20

מוֹדִיעִים Modi'in 62, 74

# N

נַפְתָּלִי Naphtali 22, 25, 26, 39, 42

נַצְרַת Nazareth 75

נֵאָפּוֹלִיס Neapolis 73

נְבוֹ Nebo 69

הַר נְבוֹ Nebo, Mt. 19

נְכוֹ Necho 53

הַנֶּגֶב Negeb 14, 19, 26

נִילוֹס Nile, R. 10, 15, 17, 58

נִינְוֵה Nineveh 11, 12, 47, 48, 51, 53

נִפּוּר Nippur 55, 56

נֹחַ Noah 10

נֹב Nob 32

# O

הַר הַזֵּיתִים Olives, Mt. of 72

אוֹן On 11

נְהַר אָרְנָת Orontes, R. 16, 47, 48

עָתְנִיאֵל Othniel 24

# P

פַּנְיוֹן Panias 58, 61, 67

מִדְבַּר פָּארָן Paran, Wilderness of 17

פַּרְתִיָה Parthian Empire 67

פַּטַלָה Patala 58

פֶּקַח Pekah 50

פֶּלָה Pella 58, 65, 73

פְּנוּאֵל Penuel 26, 45, 75

פֶּרֵיָה Perea 68, 69, 70

פֶּרְסְפּוֹלִיס Persepolis 58

פָּרַס Persian Empire 57

הַמִּפְרָץ הַפַּרְסִי Persian Gulf 58

פֶּטְרָה Petra 36, 67

פְּלֶשֶׁת Philistia 24, 27, 28, 31

פְּלִשְׁתִּים Philistines 23, 30, 31, 32, 34, 35

פִילוֹטֶרְיָה Philoteria 65

פֵּינִיקִיָה Phoenicia 46

פִּתֹם Pithom 16

פְּטוֹלְמָאִיס (עַכּוֹ) Ptolemais (Acco) 62, 67, 72, 73, 74

# Q

קַרְקַר Qarqar 47

קוּמְרָאן (מְצַד חֲסִידִים) Qumran (Mesad Hasidim) 69, 75

# R

רַבַּת בְּנֵי עַמּוֹן Rabbath-bene-ammon 36, 42, 47

רָמָה Ramah 29, 32, 45, 55, 75

רַעְמְסֵס Rameses 16, 17

רָמוֹת גִּלְעָד Ramot-gilead 42

רָפִיח Raphia 65

יַם סוּף Red Sea 58, 67

יַם סוּף Reed Sea 17

רְחֹב Rehob 22

עֵמֶק רְפָאִים Rephaim, Valley of 34

רְפִידִים Rephidim 17

רְאוּבֵן Reuben 22, 51

רְצִין Rezin 50

רִבְלָה Riblah 55

רִמּוֹן Rimmon 73

# S

יָם הַמֶּלַח Salt Sea 18

גֵּיא מֶלַח Salt, Valley of 36

שׁוֹמְרוֹן Samaria 46, 48, 49, 51, 52, 55, 58, 62, 65, 67, 68, 69, 70, 75

שׁוֹמְרוֹן סֶבַּסְטִי Samaria-Sebaste 73

שִׁמְשׁוֹן Samson 24

סַרְדִּיס Sardis 58

שָׁאוּל Saul 30, 33

סְקִיתוֹפּוֹלִיס (בֵּית שְׁאָן) Scythopolis (Beth-shean) 65

|  |  |
|---|---|
| סְקִיתוֹפּוֹלִיס נִיסָה | Scythopolis Nysa |
| סֶבַּסְטִי | Sebaste 68 |
| סֶלֶוּקְיָה | Seleucia 61, 65 |
| צִפּוֹרִי | Sepphoris 67, 72 |
| שַׁעַלְבִים | Shaalbim 22 |
| שַׁמְגַּר | Shamgar 24 |
| שָׁרוֹן | Sharon 36 |
| שְׁכֶם | Shechem 14, 15, 38, 39, 42, 44, 67, 75 |
| שֵׁם | Shem 10 |
| הַשְּׁפֵלָה | Shephelah 21, 27 |
| שִׁילֹה | Shiloh 28, 29, 75 |
| שִׁמְרוֹן | Shimron 21 |
| שׁוּנֵם | Shunem 33 |
| מִדְבַּר שׁוּר | Shur, Wilderness of 17 |
| סָאַנ | Siannu 47 |
| צִידוֹן | Sidon 22, 23 |
| צִידוֹנִים | Sidonians 31 |
| נִקְבַּת־הַשִּׁילוֹחַ | Siloam Tunnel 52 |
| שִׁמְעוֹן | Simeon 22 |
| שִׁמְעוֹן | Simon 62 |
| הַר סִינַי | Sinai, Mt. 17 |
| מִדְבַּר סִינַי | Sinai, Wilderness of 17 |
| שׂוֹכֹה | Socoh 31, 42, 52 |
| סְדֹם | Sodom 75 |
| נַחַל שׂוֹרֵק | Sorek, R. 27 |
| מִגְדַּל אַסְטְרָטוֹן | Strato's Tower 61, 65, 67 |
| סֻכּוֹת | Succoth 17, 26, 40 |
| שׁוּשָׁן | Susa 56, 58 |
| סוּרְיָה | Syria 11, 13, 16, 23, 65 |

## T

|  |  |
|---|---|
| תַּעְנַךְ | Taanach 22, 25, 42 |
| הַר תָּבוֹר | Tabor, Mt. 25 |
| תָּמָר | Tamar 40 |
| תַּפּוּחַ | Tappuach 42 |
| תַּרְשִׁישׁ | Tarshish 41 |

|  |  |
|---|---|
| תְּקֹ | Tekoa 44 |
| תֵּל | Tell Qasile 40 |
| תֵּבִי | Thebes 15 |
| טְבֶרְיָה | Tiberias 70, 72, 75 |
| נְהַר חִדֶּקֶל | Tigris, R. 10, 11, 13, 16, 47, 48, 51, 54, 55 |
| תִּמְנָע | Timnah 27, 75 |
| תִּרְצָה | Tirzah 45, 46 |
| טוֹב | Tob 36 |
| תּוֹלָע | Tola 24 |
| טְרָכוֹן | Trachonitis 68, 69, 70 |
| צוֹר | Tyre 36, 37, 40, 42, 46, 48, 58, 73, 75 |
| הַגַּיְא | Tyropoeon Valley 43 |

## U

|  |  |
|---|---|
| הַיָּם הָעֶלְיוֹן | Upper Sea 51, 56 |
| אוּר | Ur 11, 12 |
| עֻזִּיָּה | Uzziah 49 |

## V

|  |  |
|---|---|
| דֶּרֶךְ הַיָּם | Via Maris 11 |

## Z

|  |  |
|---|---|
| זַנְזִיבַּר | Zanzibar 41 |
| צָרְתָן | Zarethan 40 |
| זְבוּלוּן | Zebulun 22, 25, 26, 34, 39, 42 |
| צִיקְלַג | Ziklag 32, 33, 34, 55, 75 |
| מִדְבַּר צִן | Zin, Wilderness of 17 |
| זִיף | Ziph 32, 52 |
| מִדְבַּר זִיף | Ziph, Wilderness of 32 |
| צֹעַן | Zoan 11 |
| צוֹעַר | Zoar 19 |
| צָרְעָה | Zorah 27, 55 |

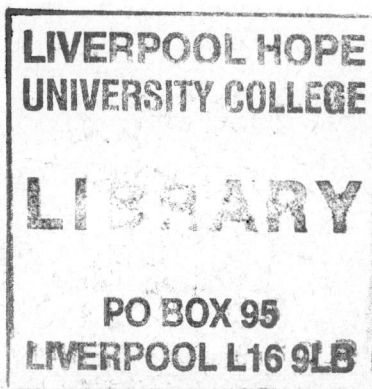